Name ______________________

Alike and Different

2

3

Directions: 1–4 Circle the flowers that are alike. Cross out the one that is different.

Copyright © Houghton Mifflin Company. All rights reserved.

Name ___________________________________

Practice 1.2

Sort by Color

1

2

3

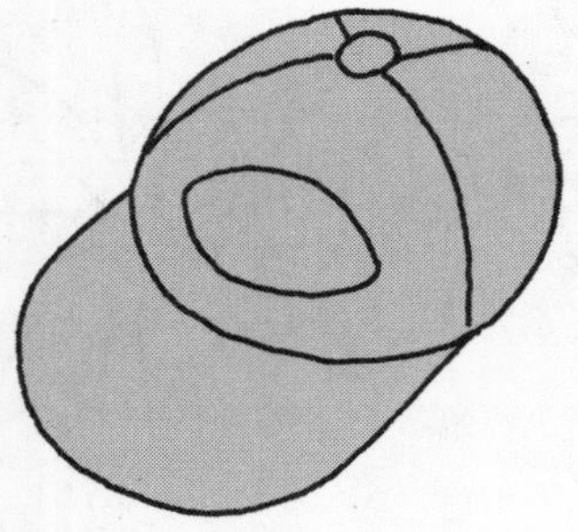
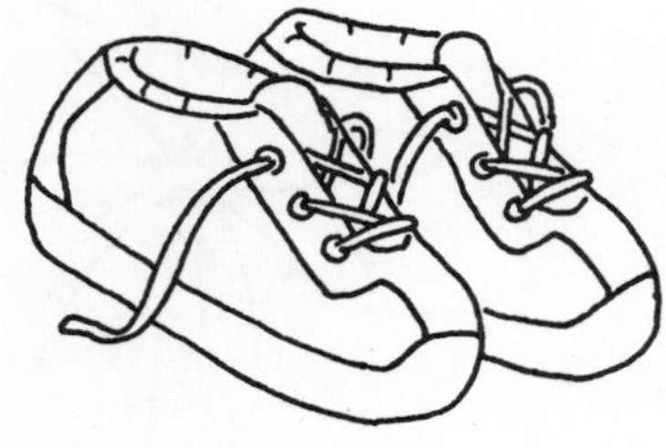
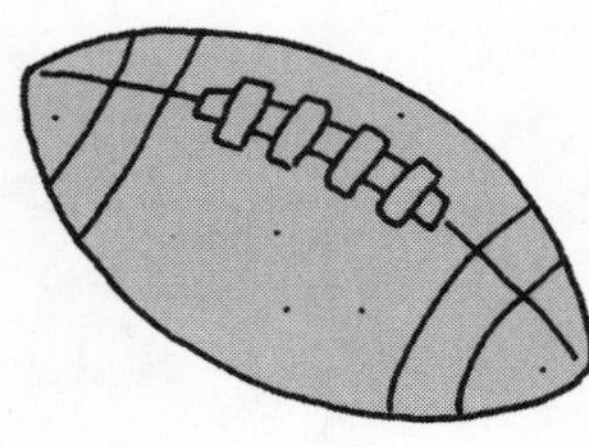

4

Directions: 1–4 Circle the pictures that are the same color.

Copyright © Houghton Mifflin Company. All rights reserved.

Name ____________________

Practice 1.3

Sort by Size

2

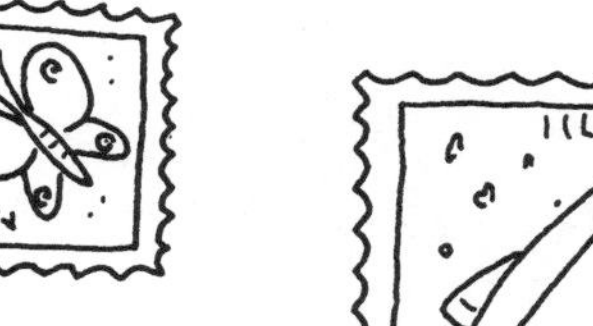

Directions: **1** Color the big coins red. **2** Color the small stamps blue.

Copyright © Houghton Mifflin Company. All rights reserved.

Name ______________________________

Sort by Shape

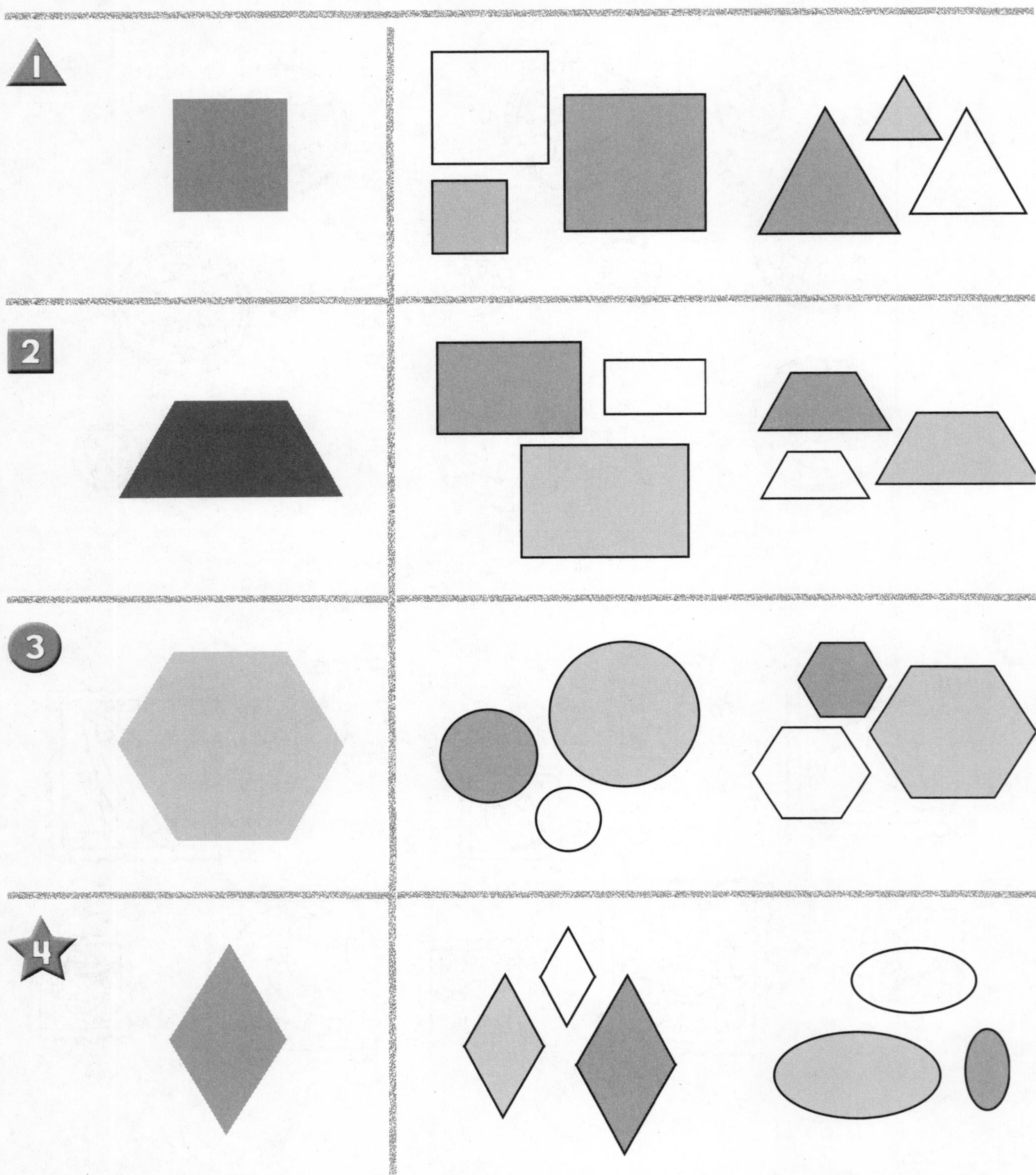

Directions: 1–4 Circle the group where the shape belongs.

Copyright © Houghton Mifflin Company. All rights reserved.

Name ______________________________

Practice 1.5

Sort by Kind

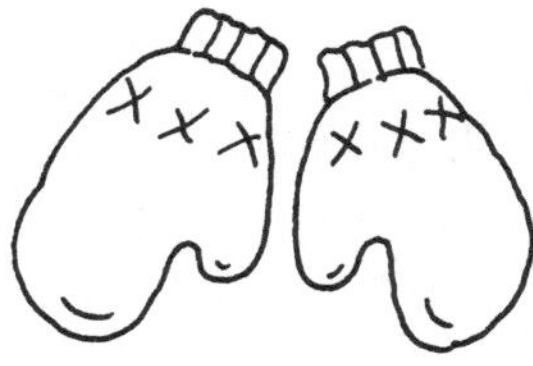

2

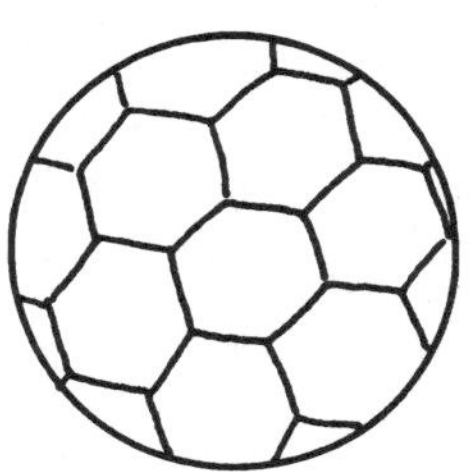
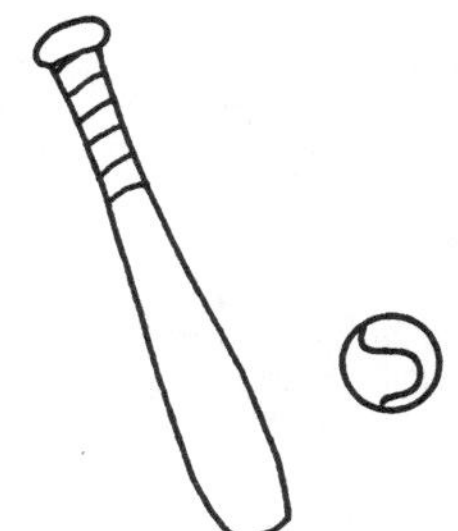

3

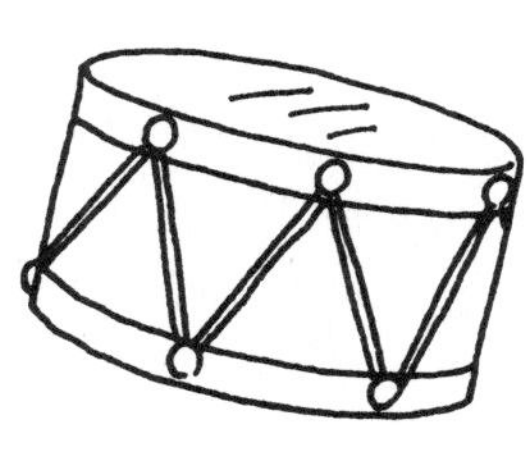
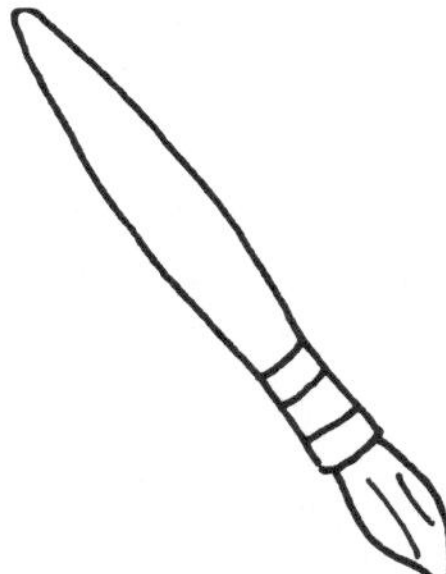
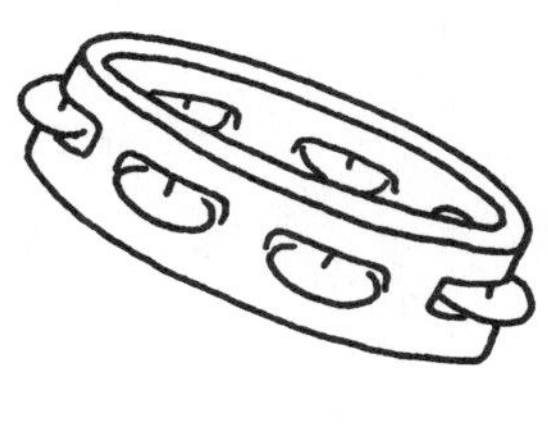

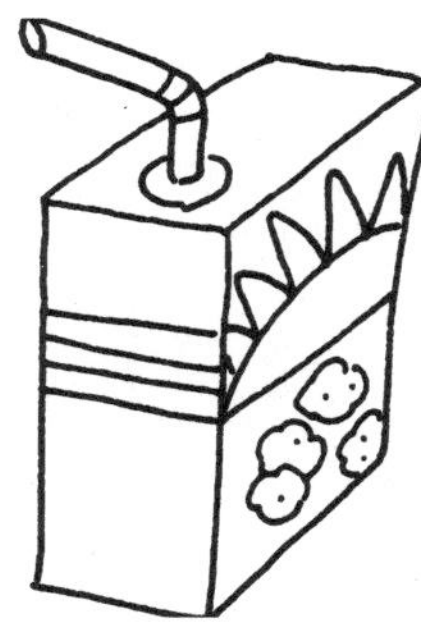
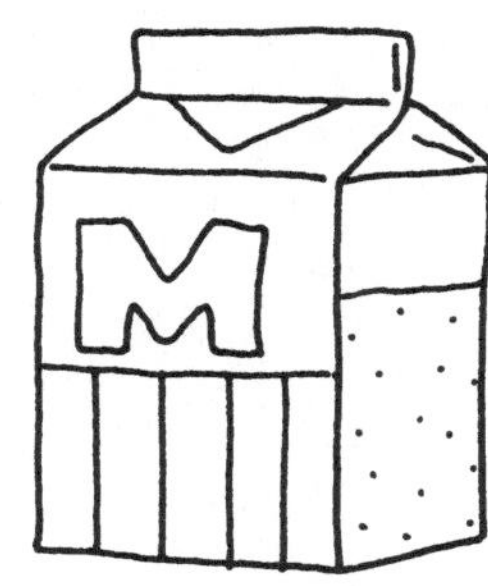

Directions: Circle the items that show: **1** things you wear, **2** games you can play, **3** things that make music, and **4** things you drink.

Copyright © Houghton Mifflin Company. All rights reserved.

Use with Teacher's Edition pages 13A–14.

Name ________________________________

Practice 1.6

Sort by Own Rule

Directions: Think of a sorting rule. Color blue the things you would put in one group. Color green the things you would put in the other group. Tell about your sorting rule.

Copyright © Houghton Mifflin Company. All rights reserved.

Use with Teacher's Edition pages 15A–16.

Name ______________________________

Practice 1.7

Problem Solving: Use Logical Reasoning

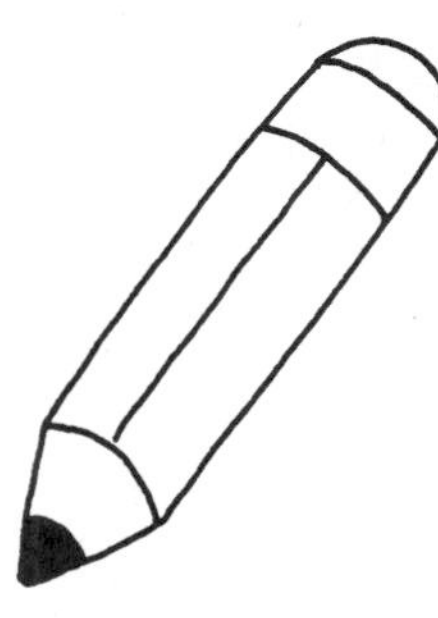
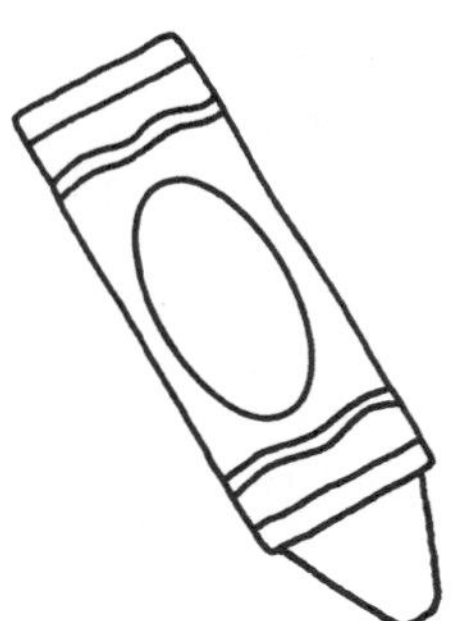

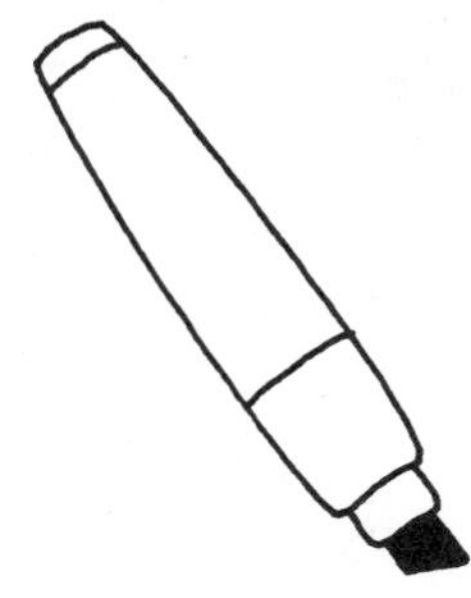

2

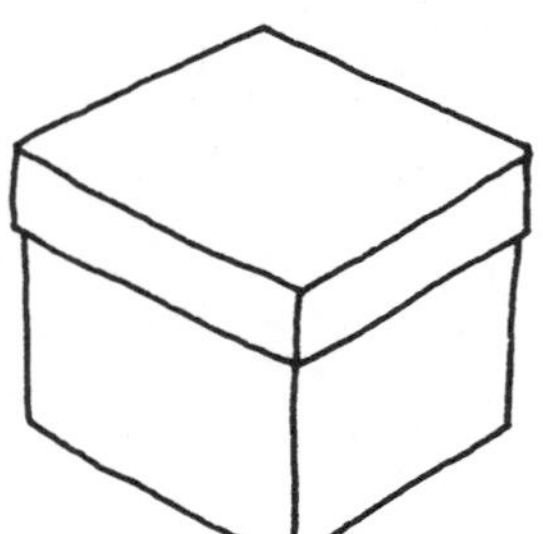

3

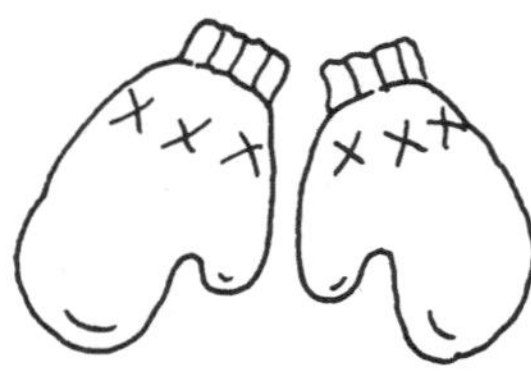

Directions: Cross out the item that does not belong in a group of: **1** thick things, **2** square things, **3** warm things, and **4** furry things.

Copyright © Houghton Mifflin Company. All rights reserved.

Use with Teacher's Edition pages 17A–18.

Name ____________________

Practice 2.1

Top, Middle, Bottom

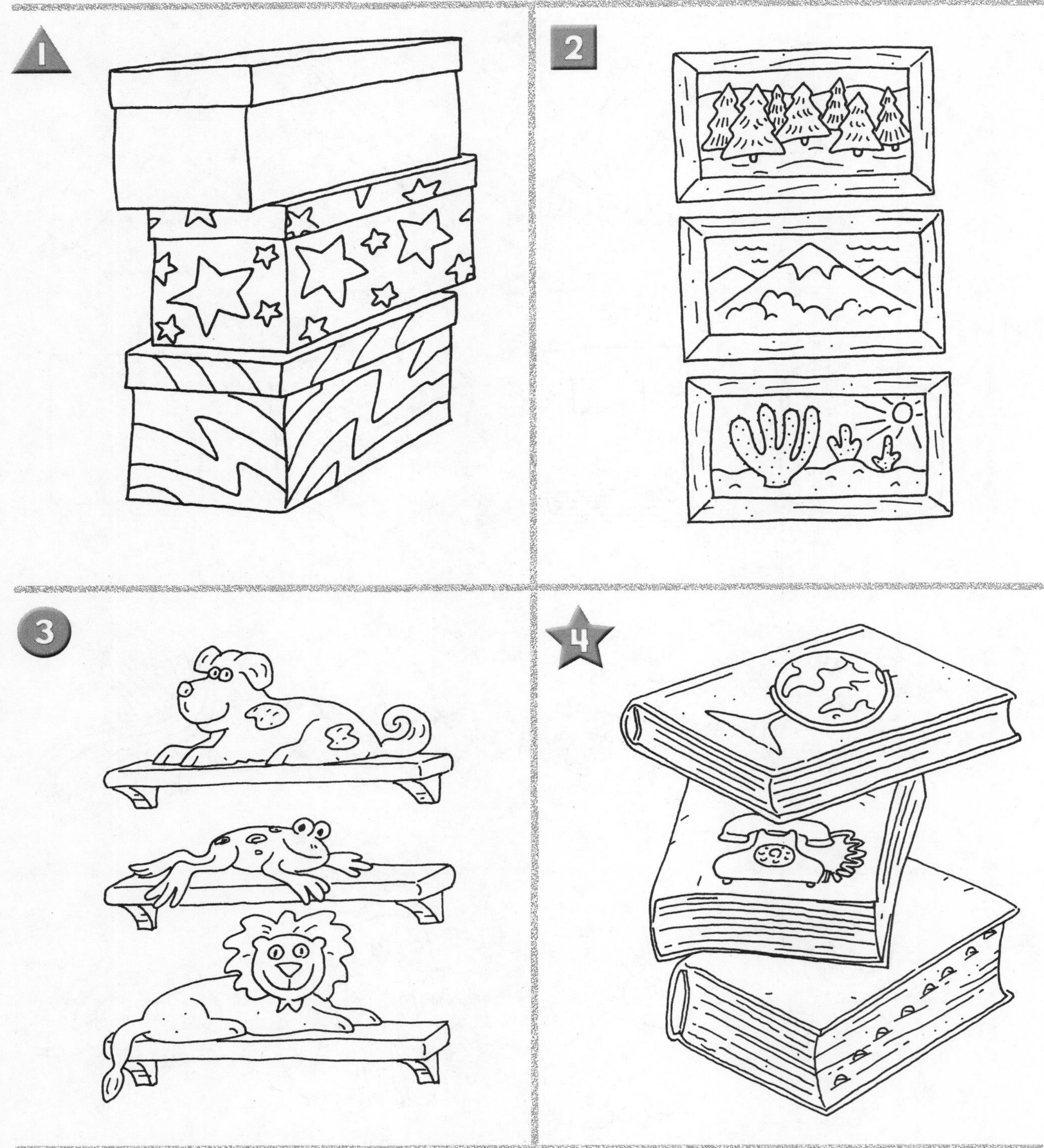

Directions: 1–4 Color the item in the middle green, the item on top red, and the item on the bottom yellow.

Copyright © Houghton Mifflin Company. All rights reserved.

Name ____________________

Practice 2.2

Before, After, Between

2

3

Directions: **1** Circle the animal that is before the one in a cap. **2** Circle the animal that is after the one in a cap. **3** Circle the animal that is before the one in a cap. **4** Circle the animal that is between the ones in caps.

Copyright © Houghton Mifflin Company. All rights reserved.

Name ____________________

Practice 2.3

Left and Right

2

3

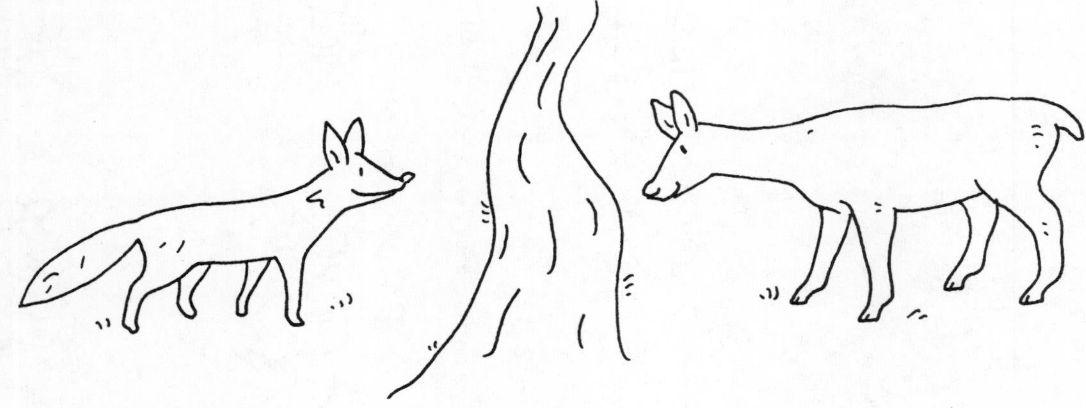

Directions: 1 Color the dog on the left blue and the one on the right red. **2** Color the tree on the left green and the one on the right yellow. **3** Color the animal on the left orange and the one on the right brown.

Copyright © Houghton Mifflin Company. All rights reserved.

Name ______________________________

Inside, Outside

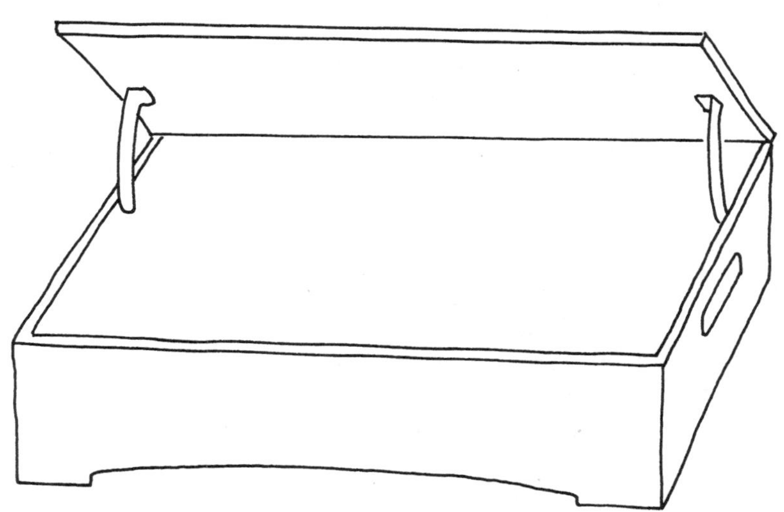

2

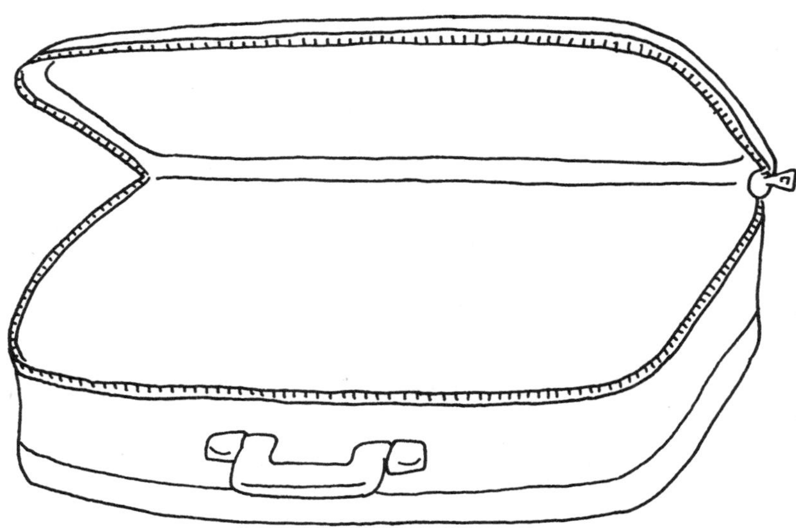

Directions: **1** Draw something blue inside the toy box. Draw something orange outside the toy box. **2** Draw something green inside the suitcase. Draw something red outside the suitcase.

Copyright © Houghton Mifflin Company. All rights reserved.

Name ______________________________

More Position Words

Directions: Color blue the child on top of the slide. Color green the child coming down. Color yellow a child walking over something. Color red a child going up. Color orange a child crawling under something.

Copyright © Houghton Mifflin Company. All rights reserved.

Name ______________________________

Practice 2.6

Patterns With Sounds and Motions

    |  

2

    |  

3

    |  

4

    |  

Directions: 1–4 Look at the pattern. Circle the picture that shows what action comes next.

Copyright © Houghton Mifflin Company. All rights reserved.

Name ___________________________

Practice 2.7

Extend Patterns

 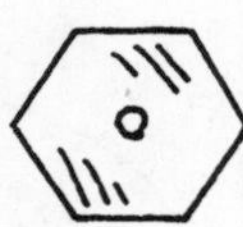  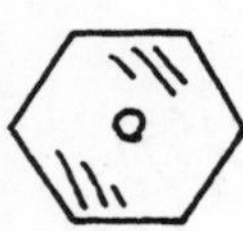   

2

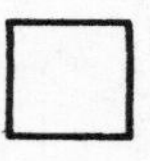 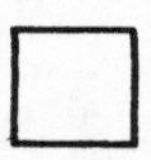  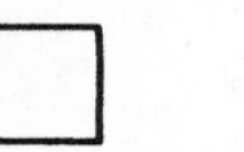  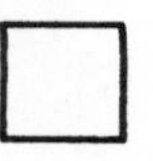 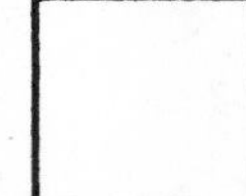

3

5

Directions: 1–5 Look at the pattern. Circle the item that is likely to come next in the pattern.

Copyright © Houghton Mifflin Company. All rights reserved.

Name ______________________

Practice 2.8

Translate Patterns

1

2

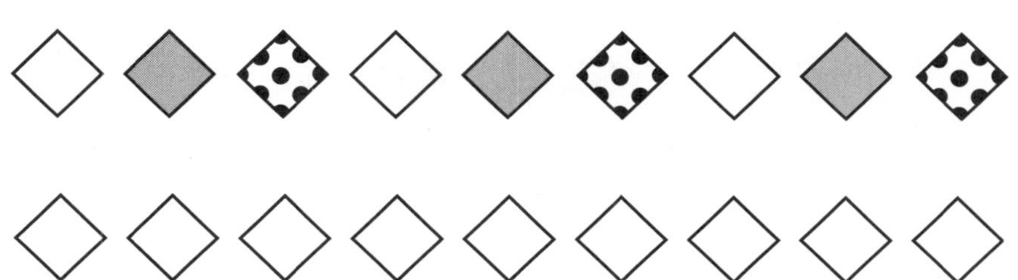

3

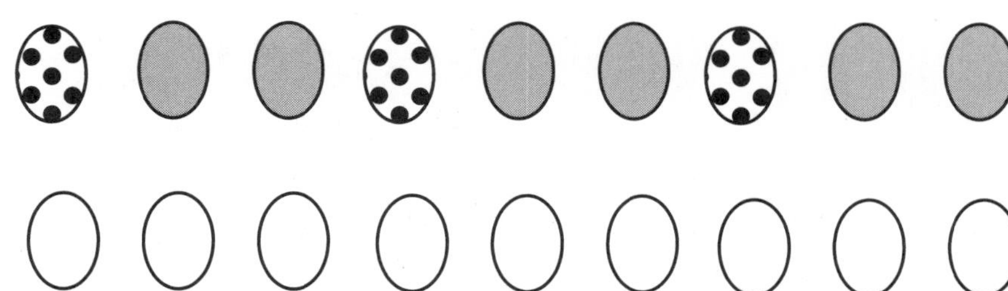

Directions: 1–3 Find the pattern. Show the same pattern using different colors.

Copyright © Houghton Mifflin Company. All rights reserved.

Name ________________________________

Practice 2.9

Problem Solving: Use a Pattern

Directions: Use pattern blocks to continue the pattern. Draw and color the blocks you used.

Copyright © Houghton Mifflin Company. All rights reserved.

Name ______________________________

Practice 3.1

Match One to One

Directions: **1–6** Draw lines to match the items one to one.

Copyright © Houghton Mifflin Company. All rights reserved.

Name ___________________________________

Practice 3.2

Same Number

 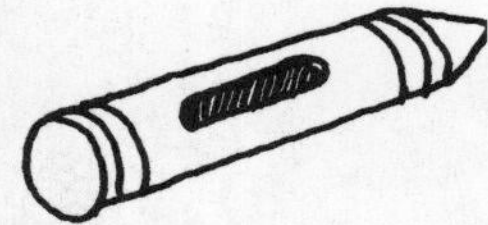 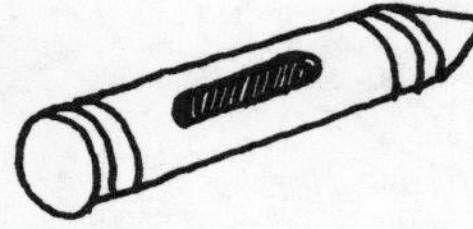 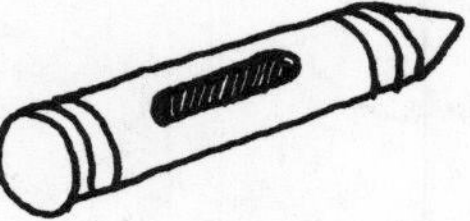

2

 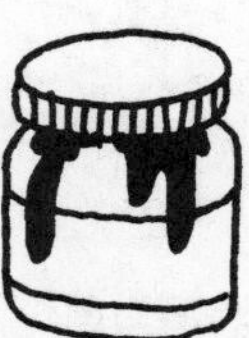

Directions: 1–4 Draw sets to show the same number of items.

Copyright © Houghton Mifflin Company. All rights reserved.

Name ______________________________

Practice 3.3

More

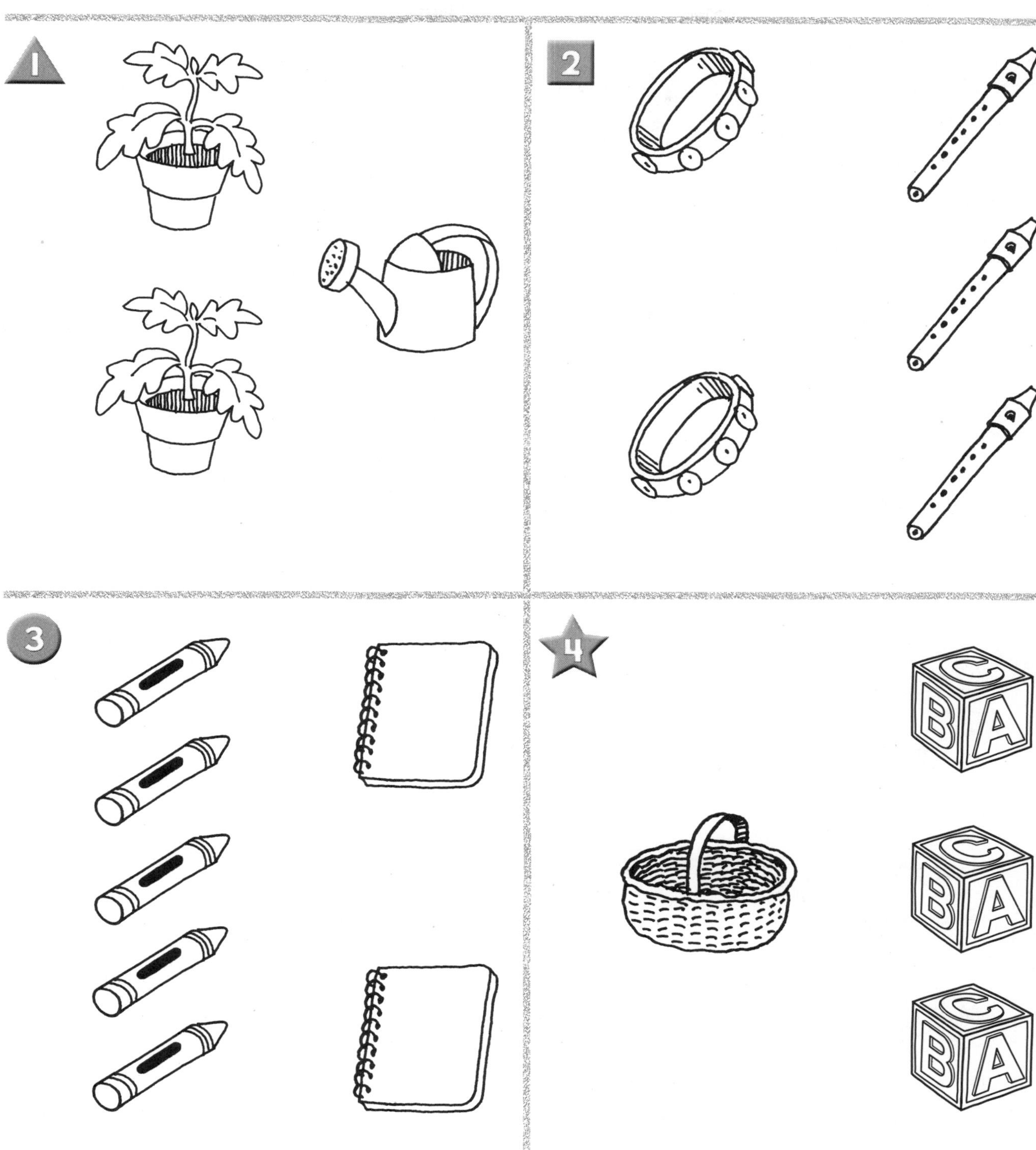

Directions: 1–4 Count the items in each set. Color the set that has more.

Copyright © Houghton Mifflin Company. All rights reserved.

Use with Teacher's Edition pages 47A–48.

Name ______________________________

Practice 3.4

Fewer

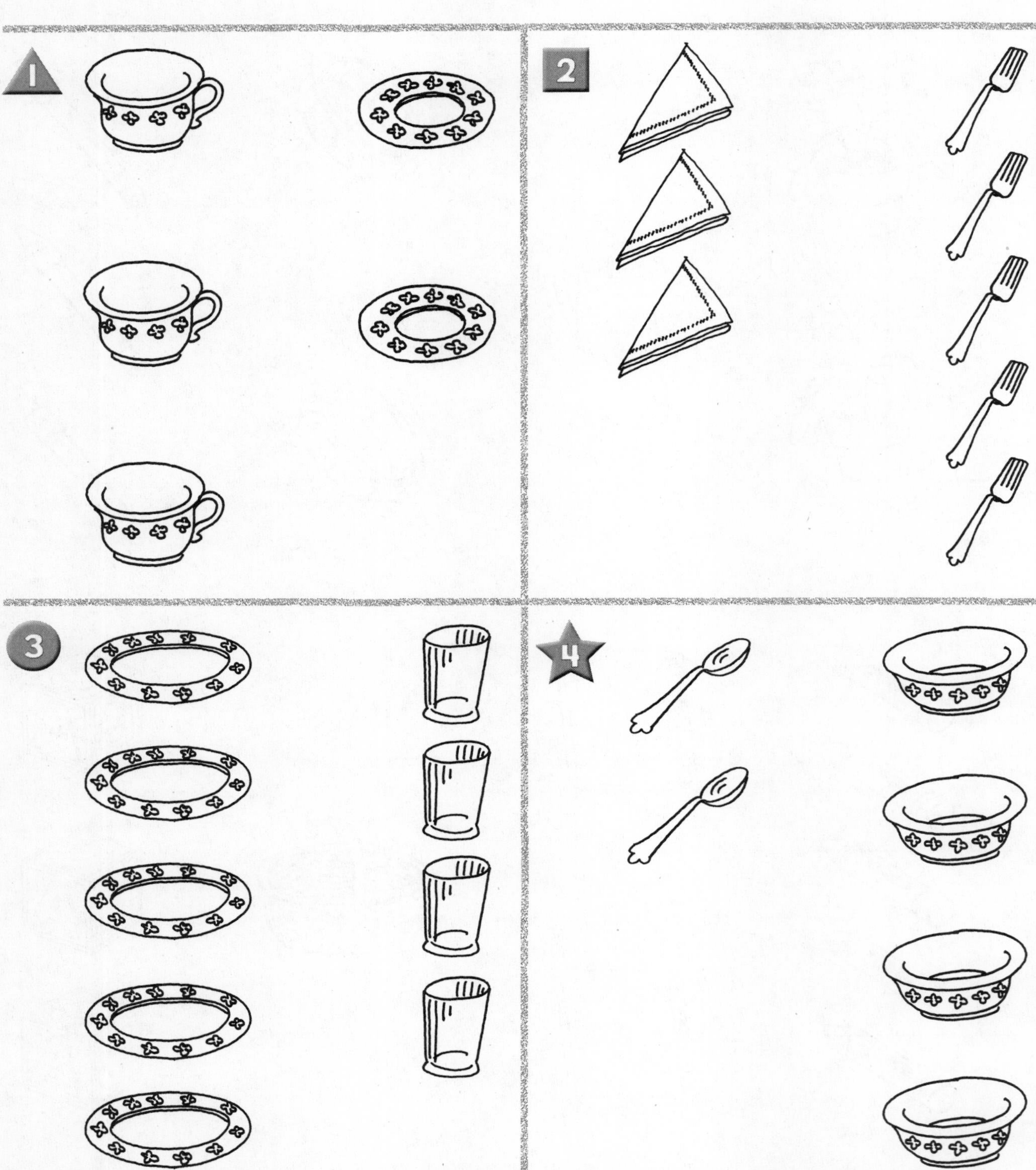

Directions: 1–4 Match the items one to one. Circle the set that has fewer.

Copyright © Houghton Mifflin Company. All rights reserved.

Use with Teacher's Edition pages 49A–50.

Name ______________________________

Practice 3.5

Sort and Graph

Cats and Dogs

Directions: Cut out the animal pictures. Sort the animals and glue them in the correct columns to make a graph.

Copyright © Houghton Mifflin Company. All rights reserved.

Name ___________________________________

Practice 3.6

Make a Real Graph

How Many of Each?

Directions: Cut out each box and paste it in the correct column.

Copyright © Houghton Mifflin Company. All rights reserved.

Use with Teacher's Edition pages 50E–50H.

Name ______________________________

Practice 3.7

Pictographs

How Many?

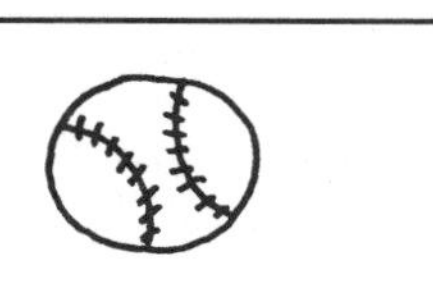	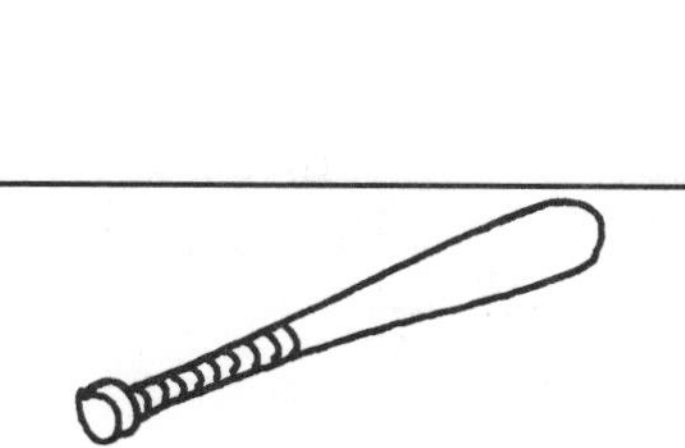	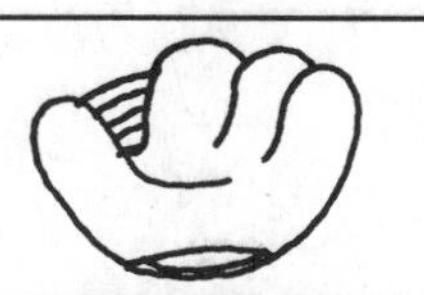

Directions: Count the items in the picture. Color the graph to show how many of each item you counted.

Copyright © Houghton Mifflin Company. All rights reserved.

Name ______________________________

Practice 3.8

Problem Solving: Use a Graph

Ways to Get to School

STOP

SCHOOL

(shoes)	(bus)	(car)

Directions: Look at the picture. Color the graph to show how each child in the picture gets to school.

Copyright © Houghton Mifflin Company. All rights reserved.

Name ______________________

Practice 4.1

One and Two

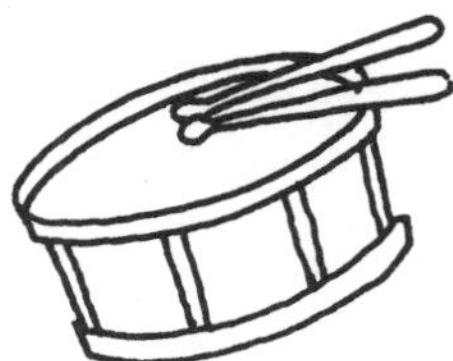

Directions: 1–5 Count the items and write the number.

Copyright © Houghton Mifflin Company. All rights reserved.

Name ______________________

Three

1

2

3

4

5

6

Directions: 1–6 Count each set and write the number. Then color each set of three.

Copyright © Houghton Mifflin Company. All rights reserved.

Name ____________________

Practice 4.3

Four

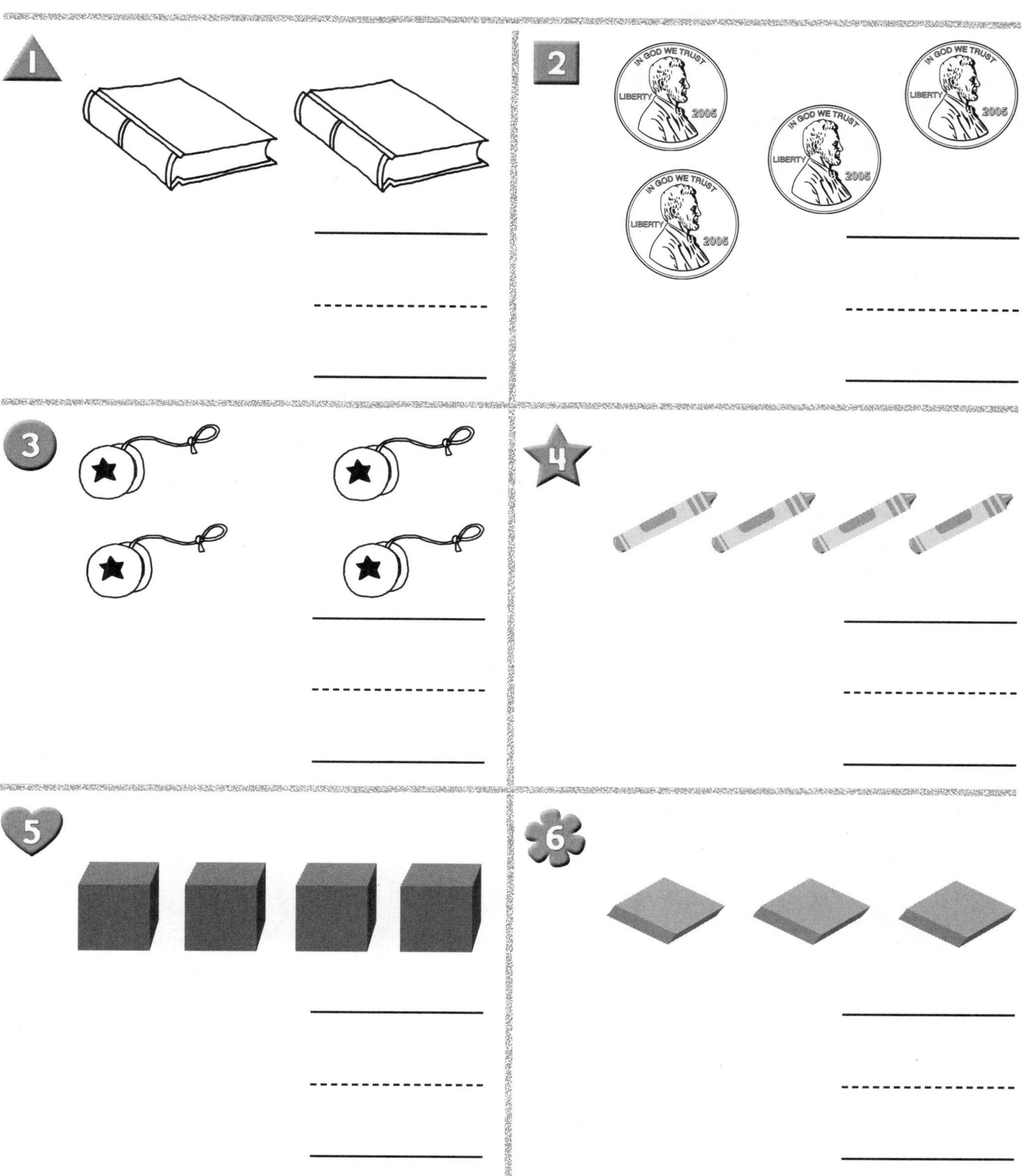

Directions: 1–6 Count each set and write the number. Then color each set of four.

Copyright © Houghton Mifflin Company. All rights reserved.

Name ______________________

Practice 4.4

Five

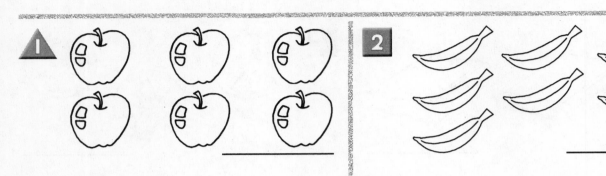

1

2

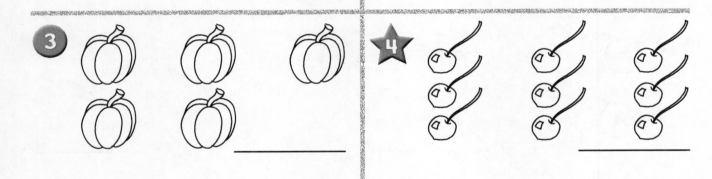

3

4

5

6

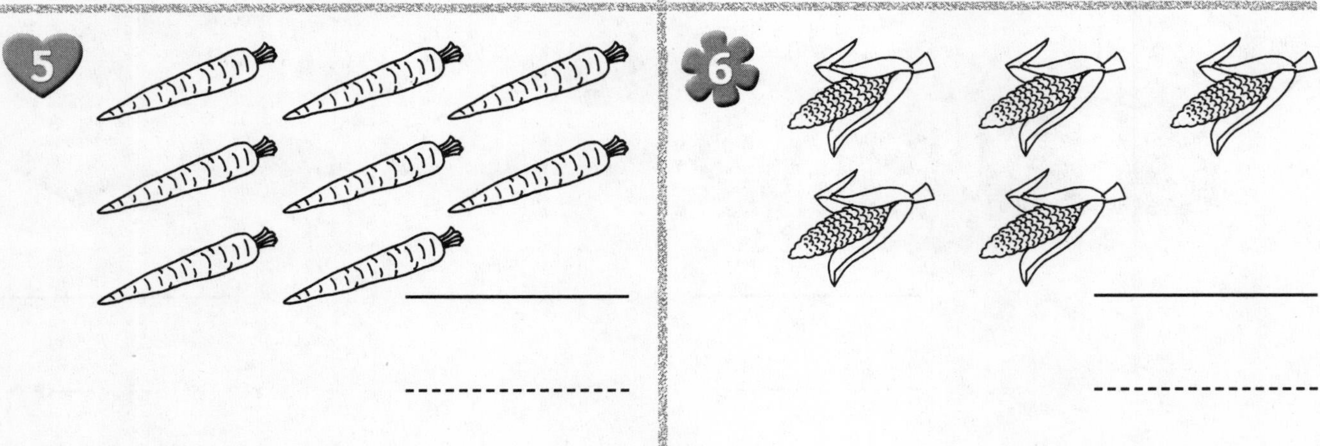

Directions: 1–6 Color five items in the set. Then write the number 5.

Copyright © Houghton Mifflin Company. All rights reserved.

Name ____________________

Practice 4.5

Zero

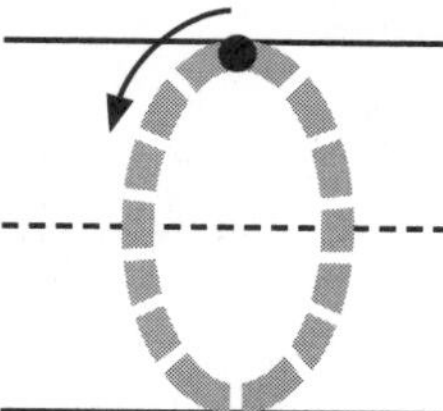

2

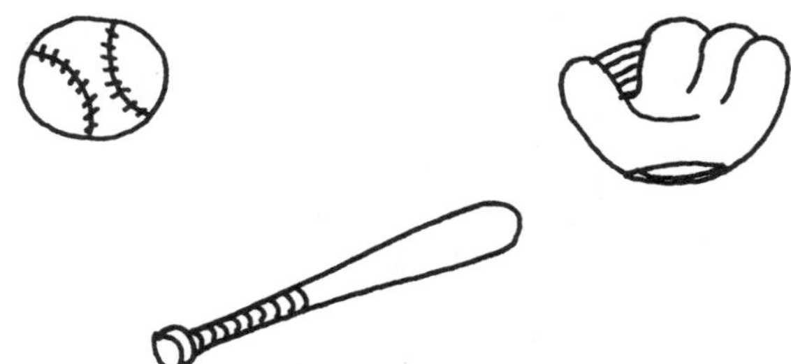

3

4

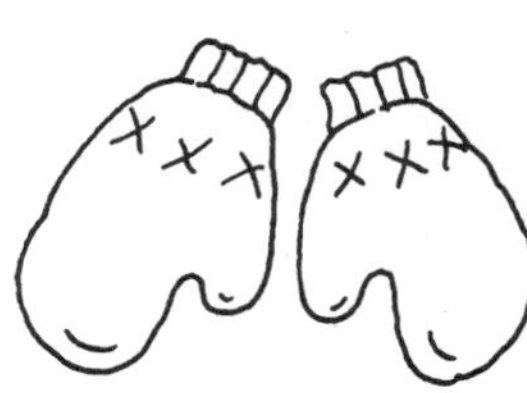

Directions: 1–4 Write how many of the item are in the picture.

Copyright © Houghton Mifflin Company. All rights reserved.

Name ______________________

Practice 4.6

Using 0–5

1

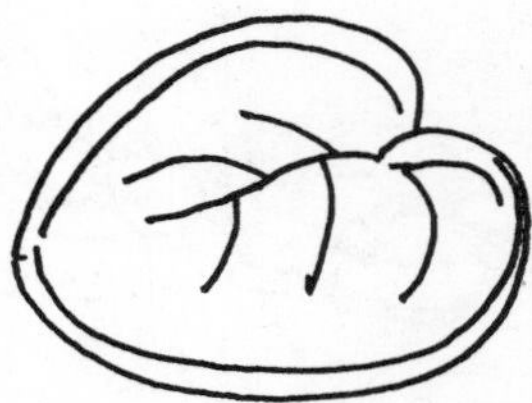

2

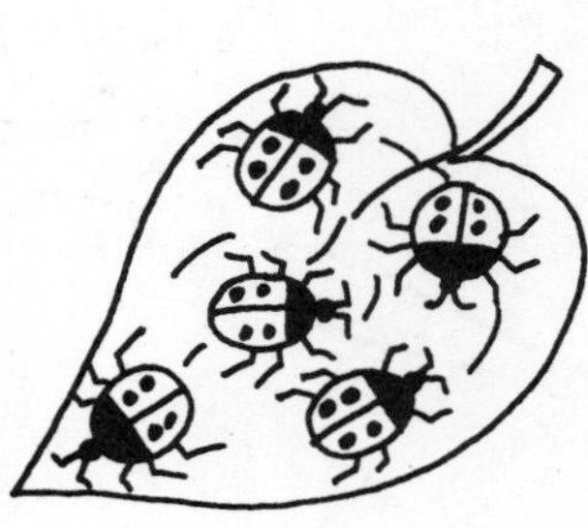

3

4

Directions: 1–4 Write the number that shows how many items.

Copyright © Houghton Mifflin Company. All rights reserved.

Name ______________________________

Practice 4.7

Problem Solving: Use Logical Reasoning

1 2 3 4 5

2

1 2 3 4 5

3

0 1 2 3 4 5

0 1 2 3 4 5

Directions: Listen to each clue. Cross out what does not match. Circle what matches all the clues. **1** Find more than 3. It is fewer than 5. **2** Find more than 1. It is between 2 and 4. **3** Find fewer than 3. It comes before 1. **4** Find fewer than 2. It is NOT 0.

Copyright © Houghton Mifflin Company. All rights reserved.

Name ______________________________

Practice 4.8

Ordinal Numbers

2

3

Directions: **1** Circle the third kitten. **2** Circle the second mouse. **3** Circle the fourth frog. **4** Circle the first fish.

Copyright © Houghton Mifflin Company. All rights reserved.

Name ____________________

Practice 5.1

Circle and Rectangle

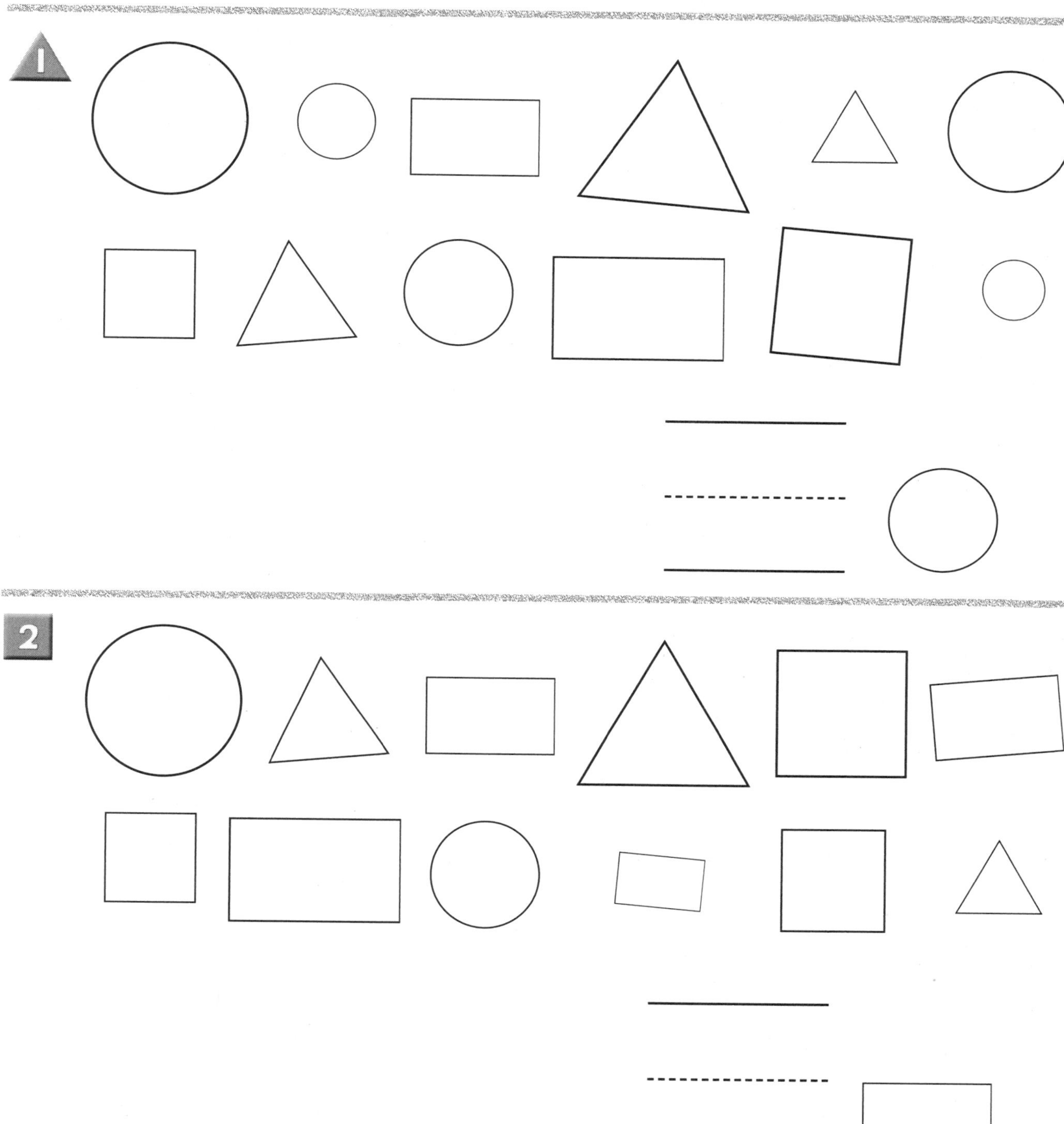

Directions: **I** Color the circles yellow. Write the number. **2** Color the rectangles green. Write the number.

Copyright © Houghton Mifflin Company. All rights reserved.

Name ______________________

Practice 5.2

Square and Triangle

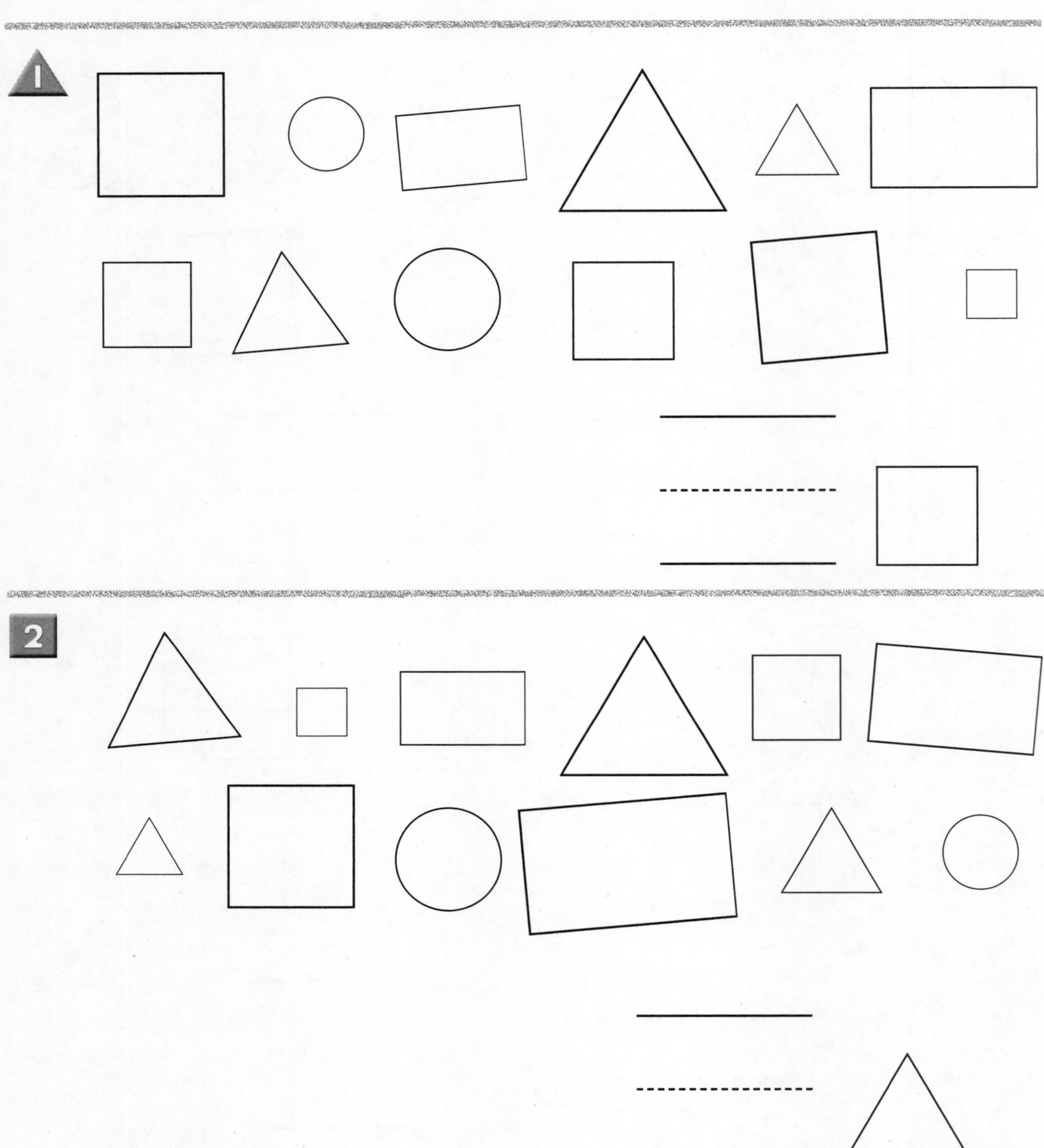

Directions: **1** Color the squares yellow. Write the number. **2** Color the triangles blue. Write the number.

Copyright © Houghton Mifflin Company. All rights reserved.

Name ______________________________

Practice 5.3

Patterns With Shapes and Positions

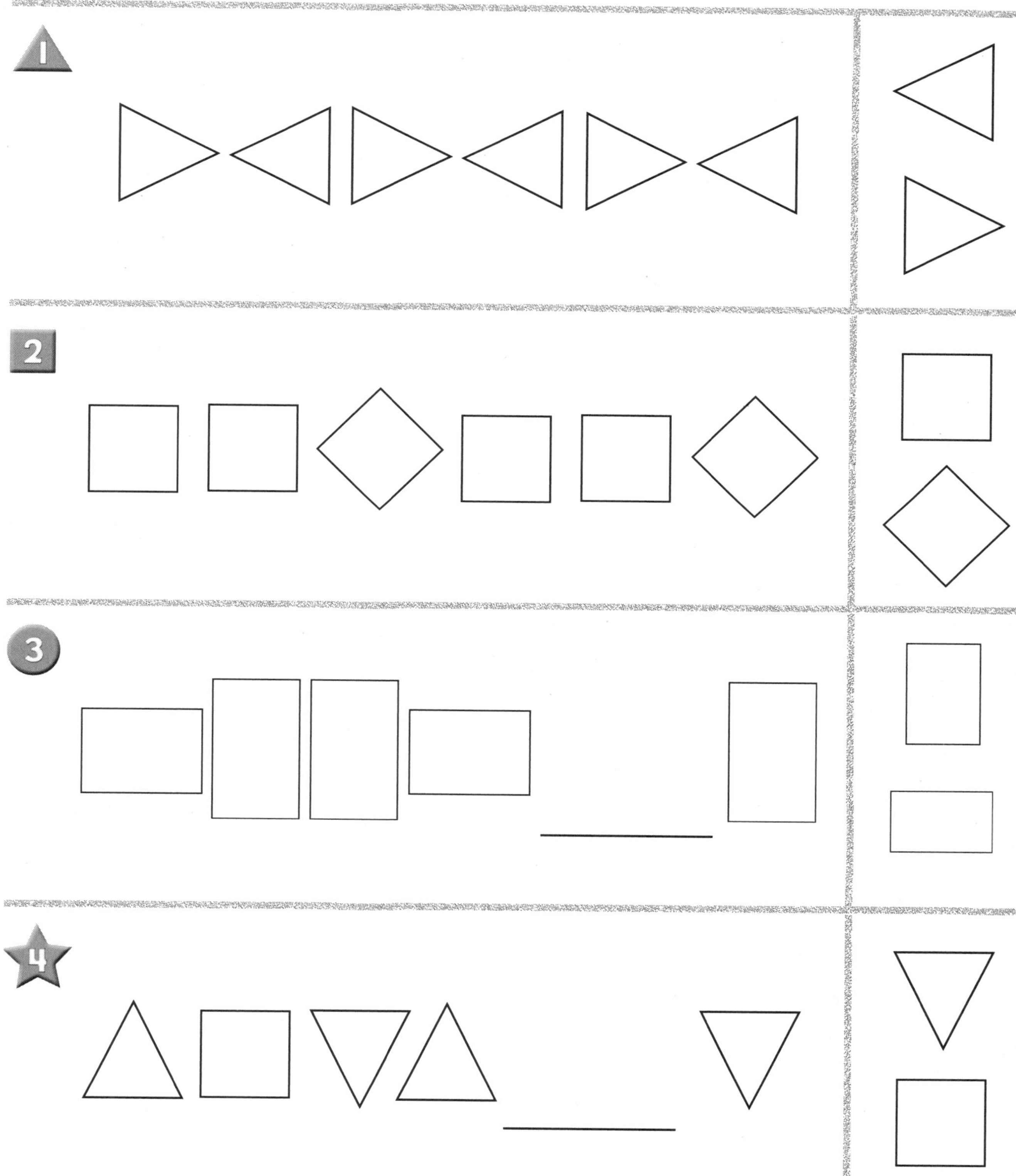

Directions: 1–2 Circle the shape that is likely to come next. **3–4** Circle the missing shape.

Copyright © Houghton Mifflin Company. All rights reserved.

Use with Teacher's Edition pages 89A–90.

Name ______________________________

Practice 5.4

Combine Plane Shapes

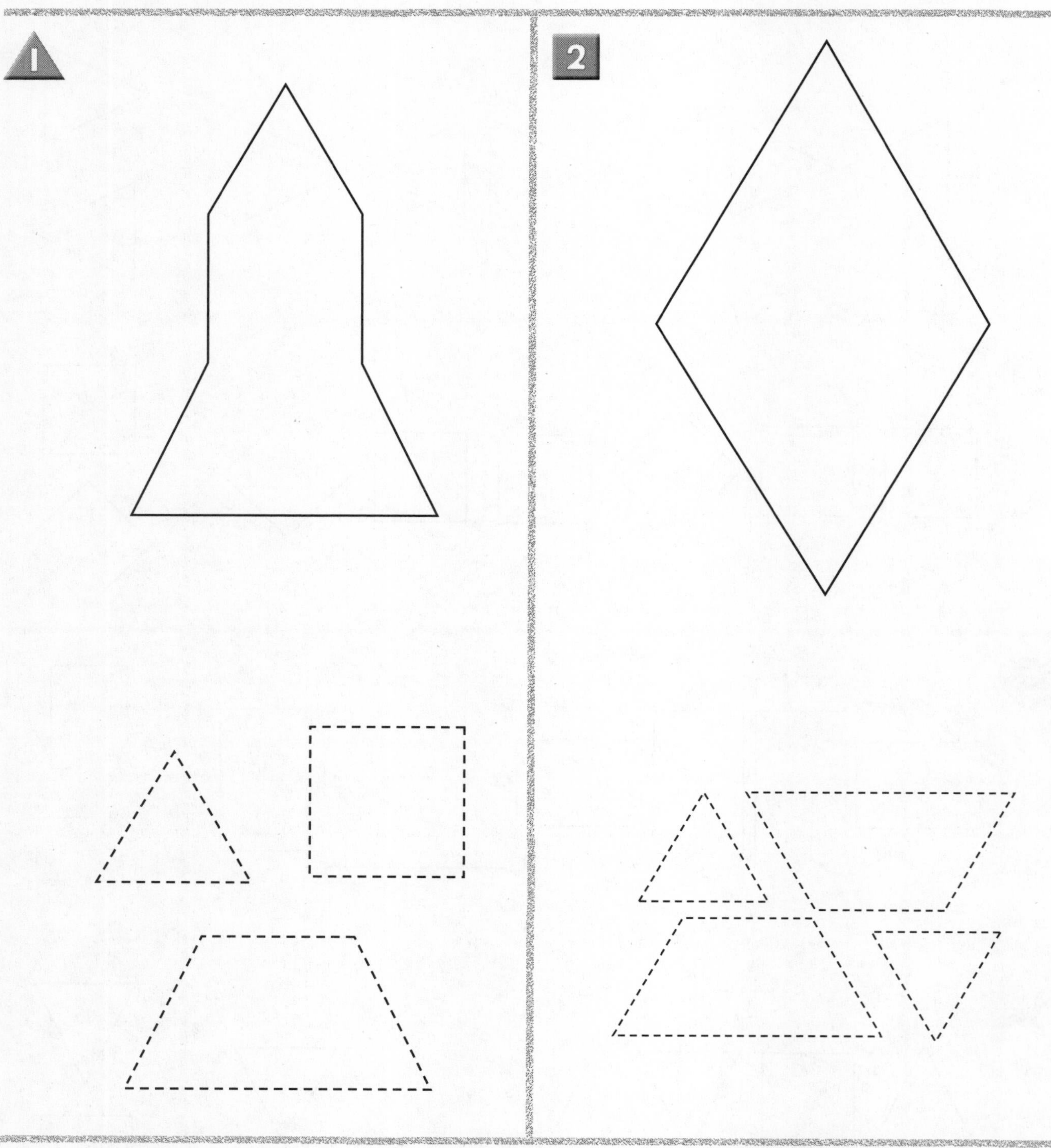

Directions: 1–2 Cut out the shapes. Combine them to make each figure. Paste them to show the shape.

Copyright © Houghton Mifflin Company. All rights reserved.

Name ____________________

Practice 5.5

Symmetry

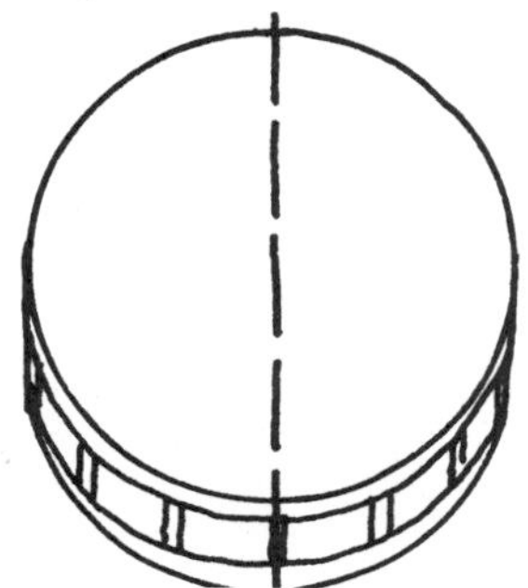
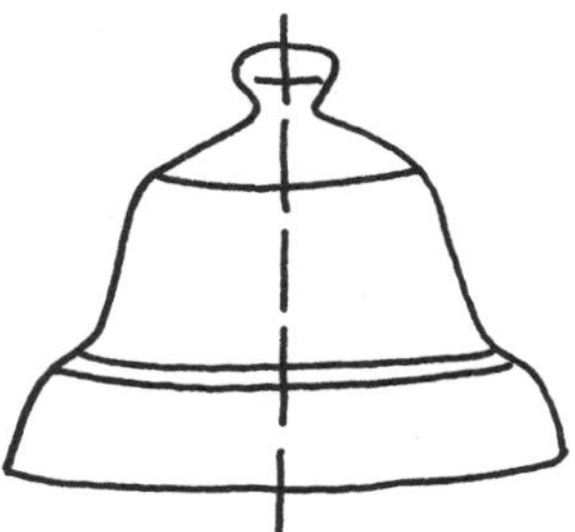
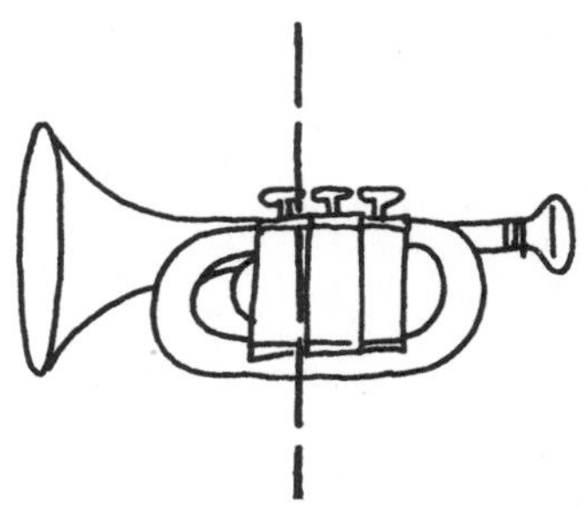

2

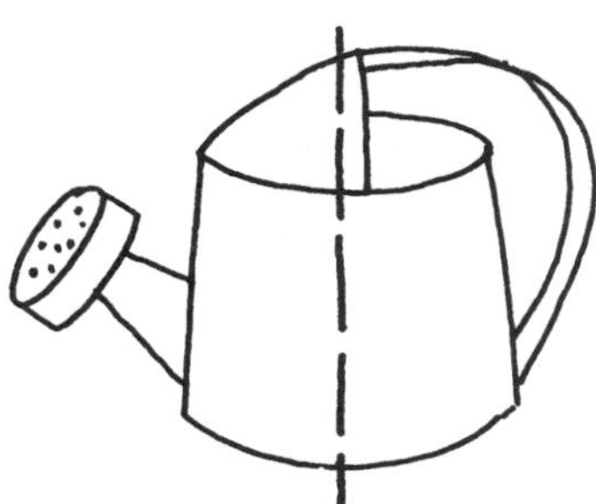

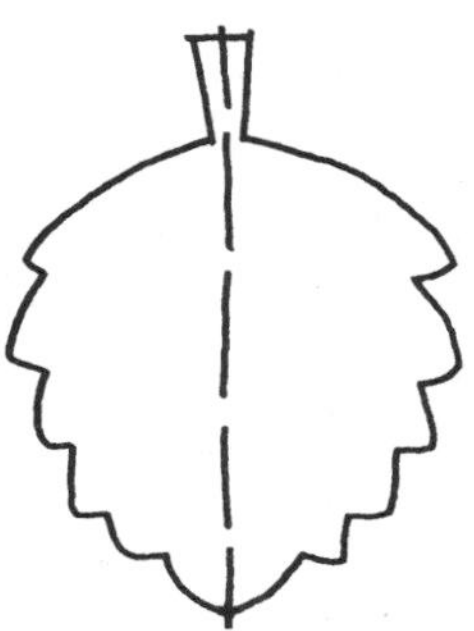

3

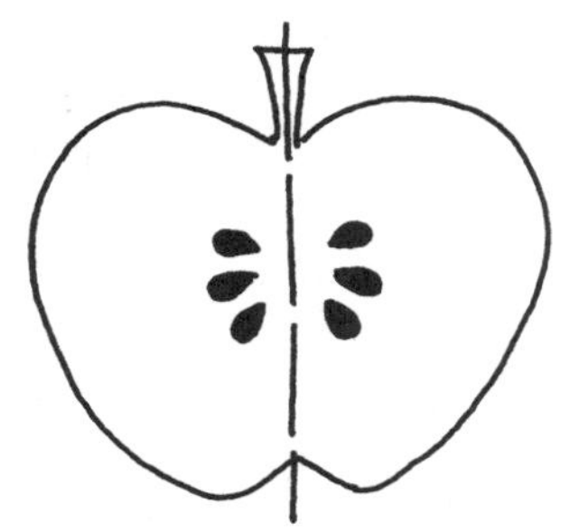
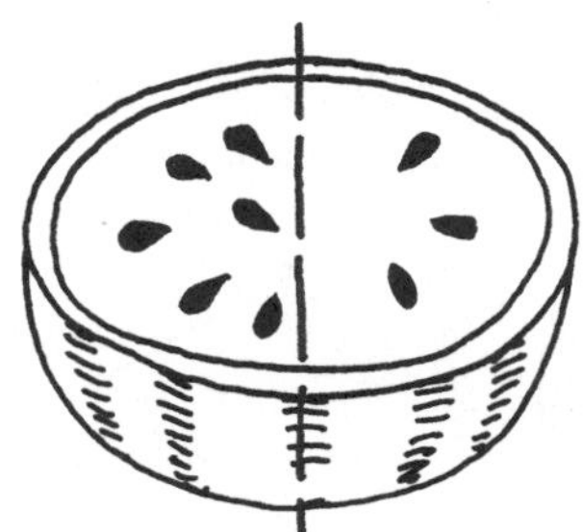

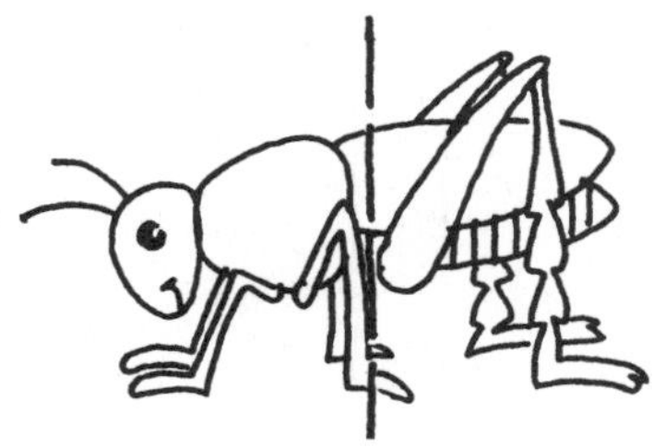

Directions: 1–4 Circle the ones with symmetry.

Copyright © Houghton Mifflin Company. All rights reserved.

Use with Teacher's Edition pages 91A–92.

Name ______________________________

Practice 5.6

Equal Parts

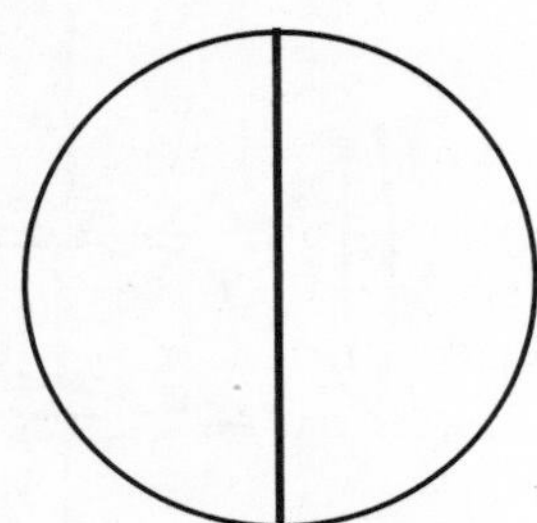

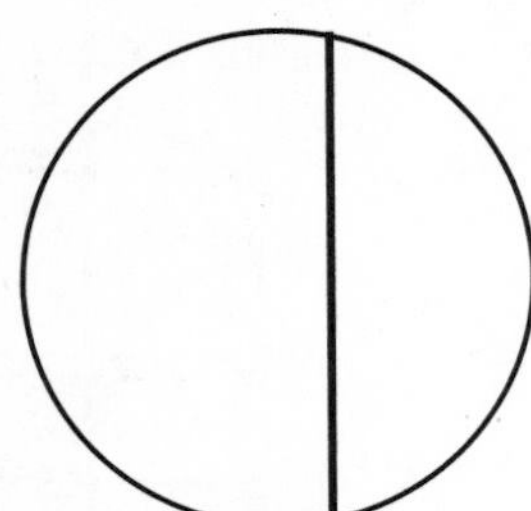

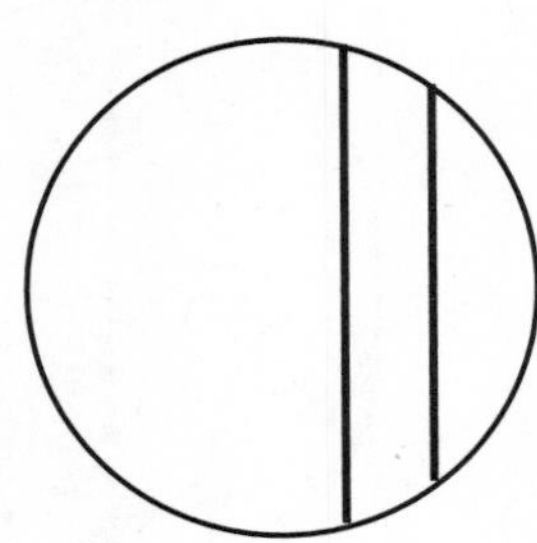

2

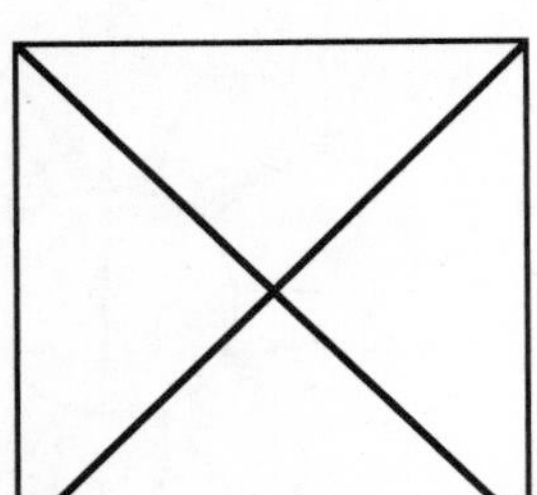

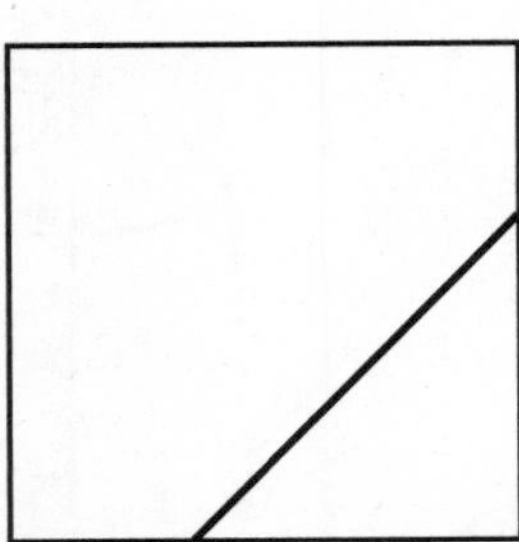

3

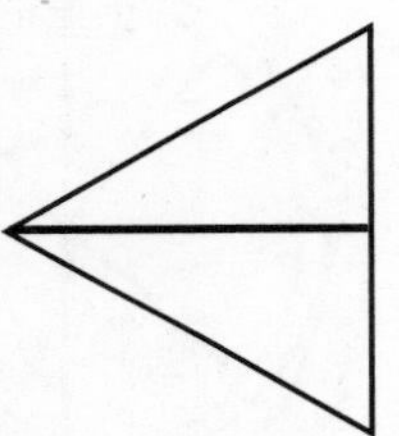

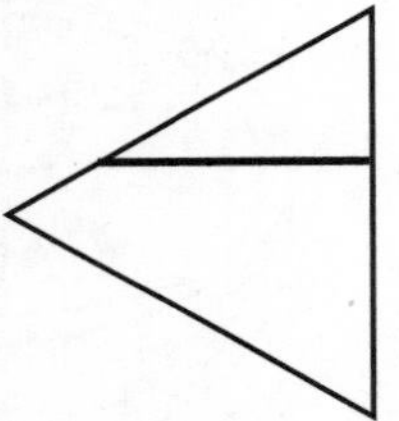

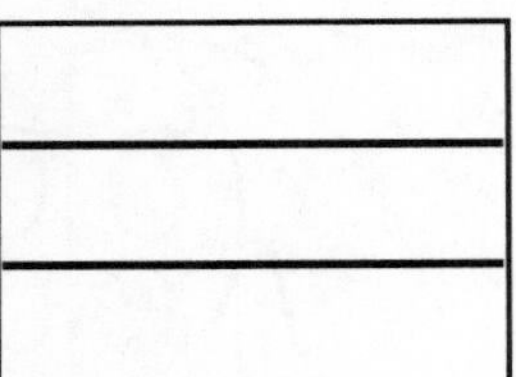

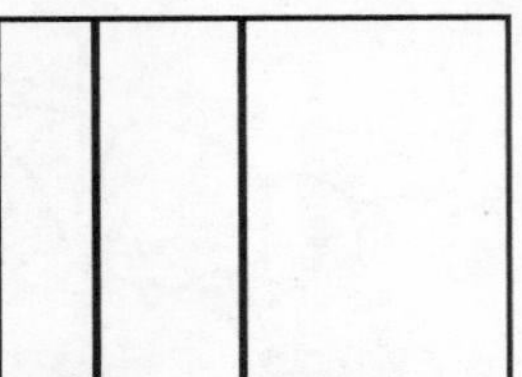

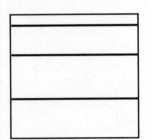

Directions: **1–4** Circle the one that shows equal parts.

Copyright © Houghton Mifflin Company. All rights reserved.

Use the Teacher's Edition pages 93A–94.

Name ______________________

Practice 5.7

Halves

Directions: Circle the foods that show halves.

Copyright © Houghton Mifflin Company. All rights reserved.

Name ______________________________

Practice 5.8

Problem Solving: Use a Picture

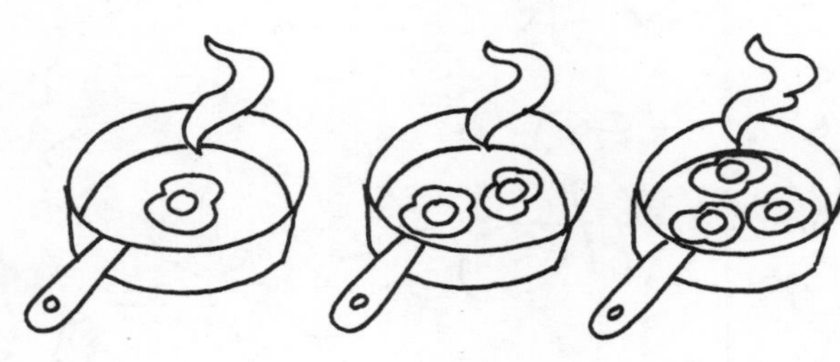

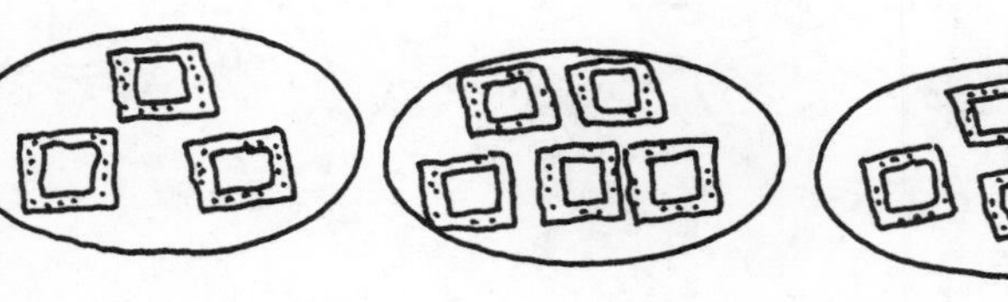

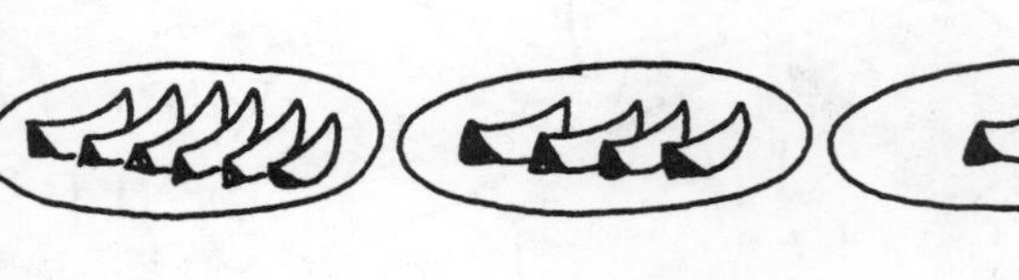

Directions: 1–4 Count the people shown. Circle the food that would give each person an equal part.

Copyright © Houghton Mifflin Company. All rights reserved.

Name ______________________________

Practice 5.9

Likely and Unlikely

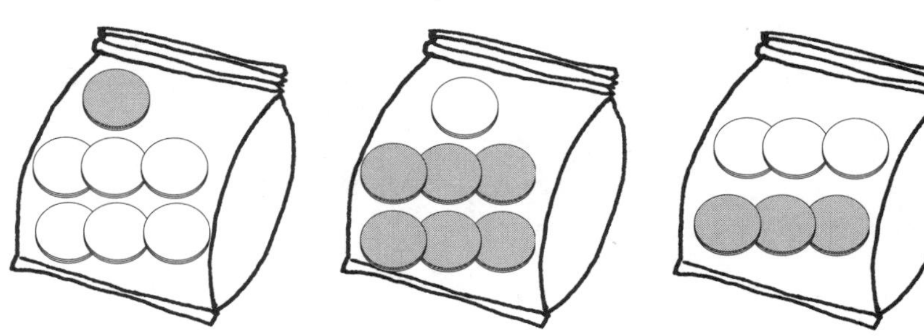

2

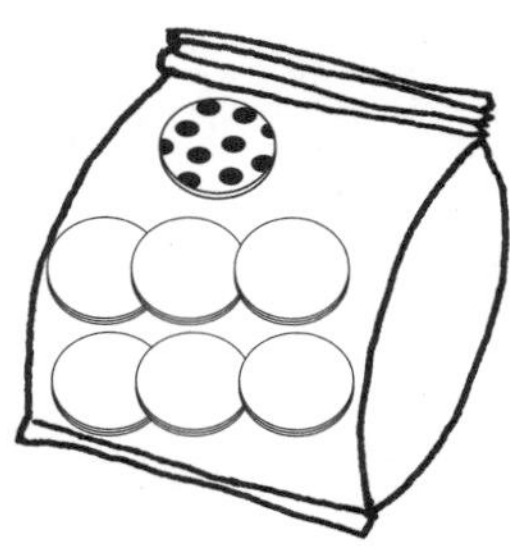

3

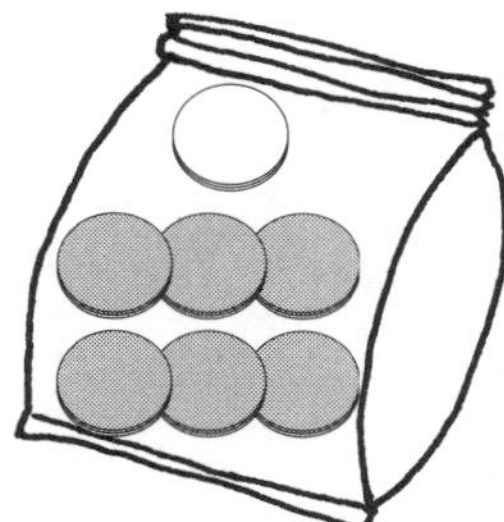

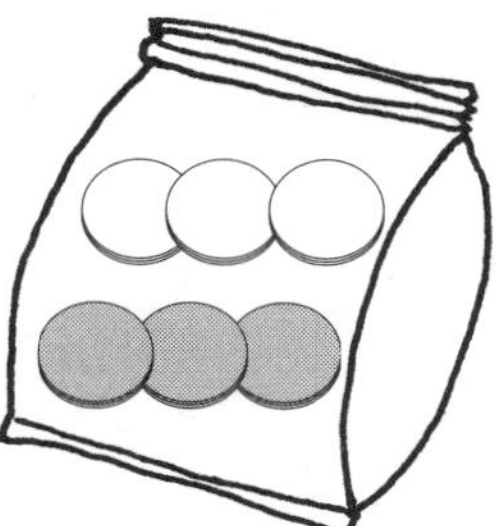

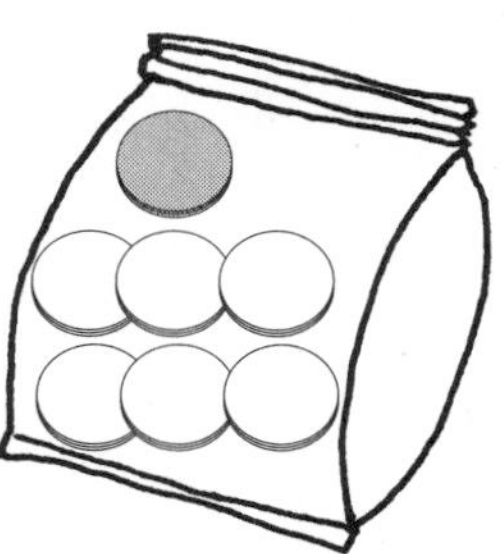

Directions: Circle the bag from which you are **1** most likely to pick a white counter, **2** least likely to pick a dotted counter, and **3** equally likely to pick a gray counter.

Copyright © Houghton Mifflin Company. All rights reserved.

Name ______________________________

Practice 5.10

Predict and Record Outcomes

Color	Predict	Record
(white)		
(gray)		
(dotted)		

Directions: Predict how many times the spinner will land on each color if you spin six times. Make a tally mark after each spin. Write the numbers of tally marks.

Copyright © Houghton Mifflin Company. All rights reserved.

Name ______________________________

Practice 6.1

Sort Solid Shapes

 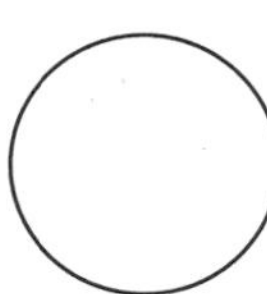 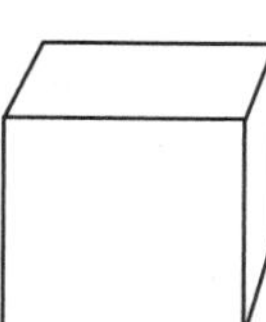 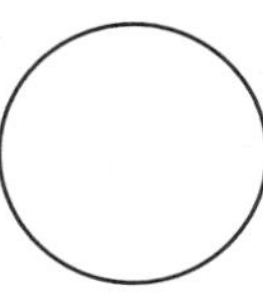

2

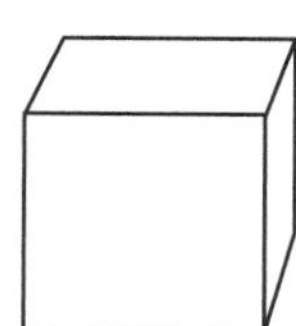  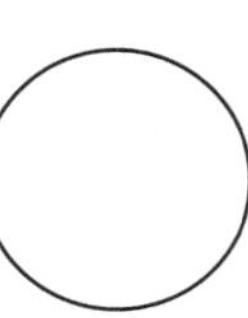 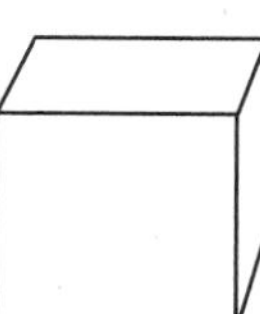 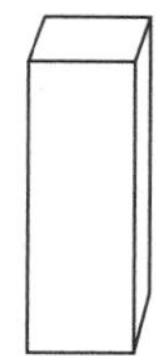

3

   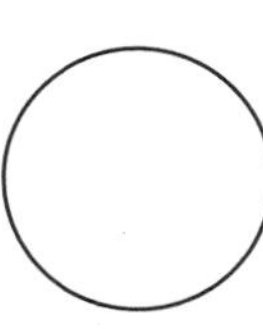 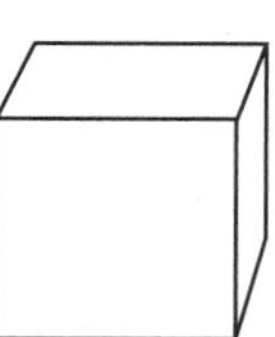 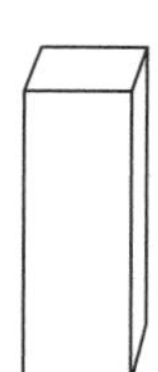

4

 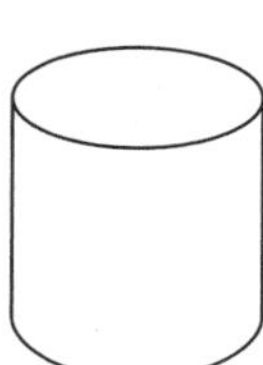 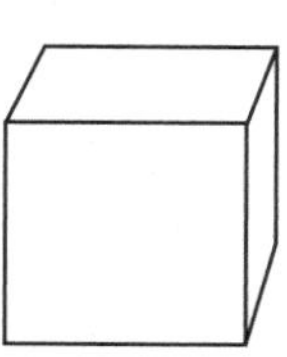 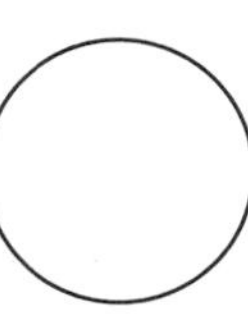 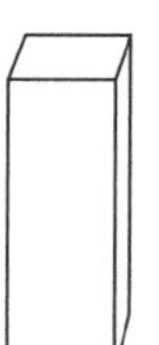 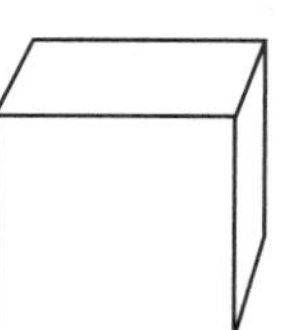

Directions: 1–4 Color the shapes that have corners orange. Color the shapes that have curves green.

Copyright © Houghton Mifflin Company. All rights reserved.

Name ______________________________

Identify Solid Shapes

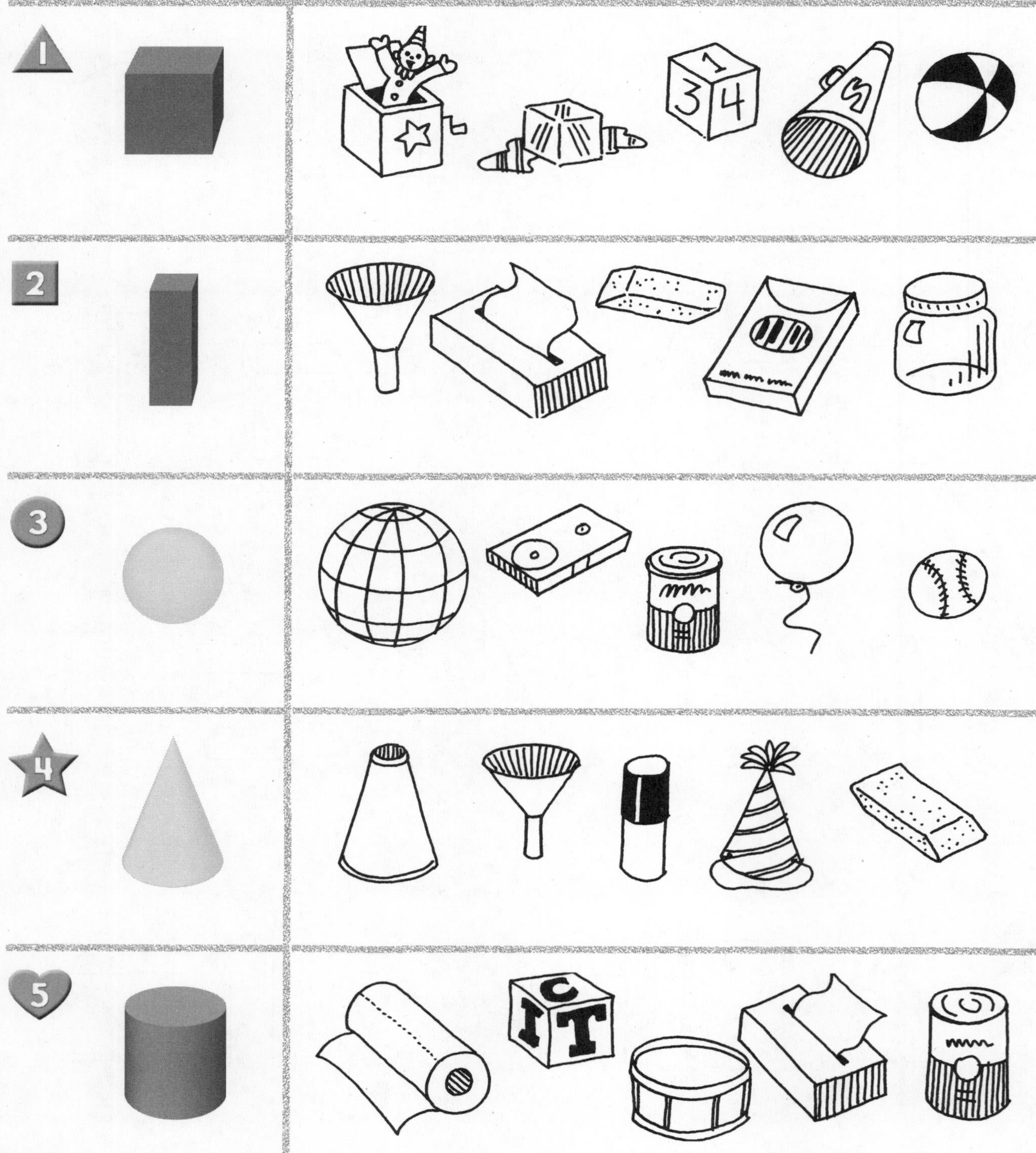

Directions: 1–5 Name and describe the solid shapes. Circle the objects that are the same shape.

Copyright © Houghton Mifflin Company. All rights reserved.

Name ___________________________

Practice 6.3

Build Solid Shapes

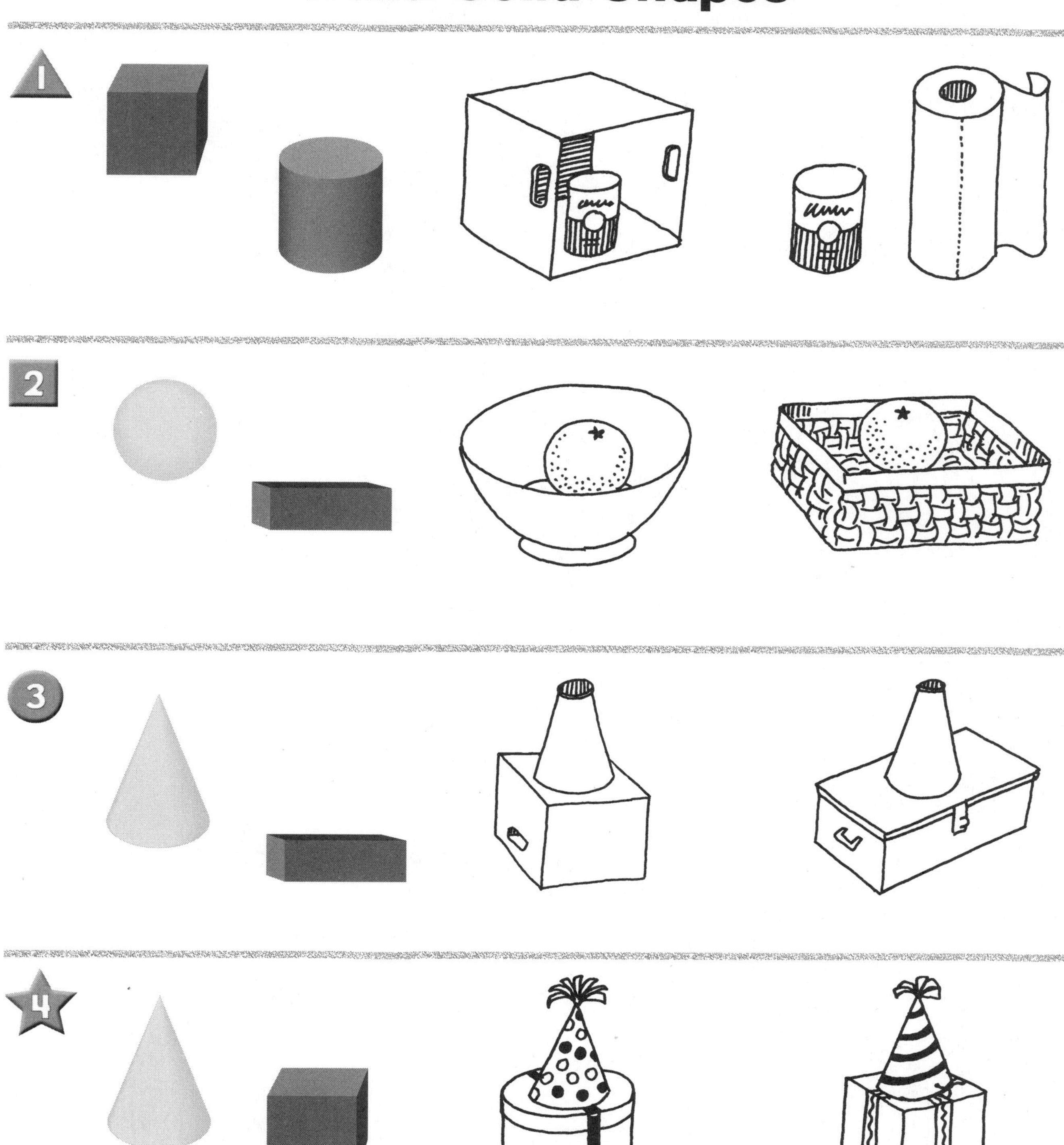

Directions: 1–4 Look at the solids. Circle the picture that has the same shapes.

Copyright © Houghton Mifflin Company. All rights reserved.

Name ______________________________

Practice 6.4

Surfaces of Solid Shapes

1

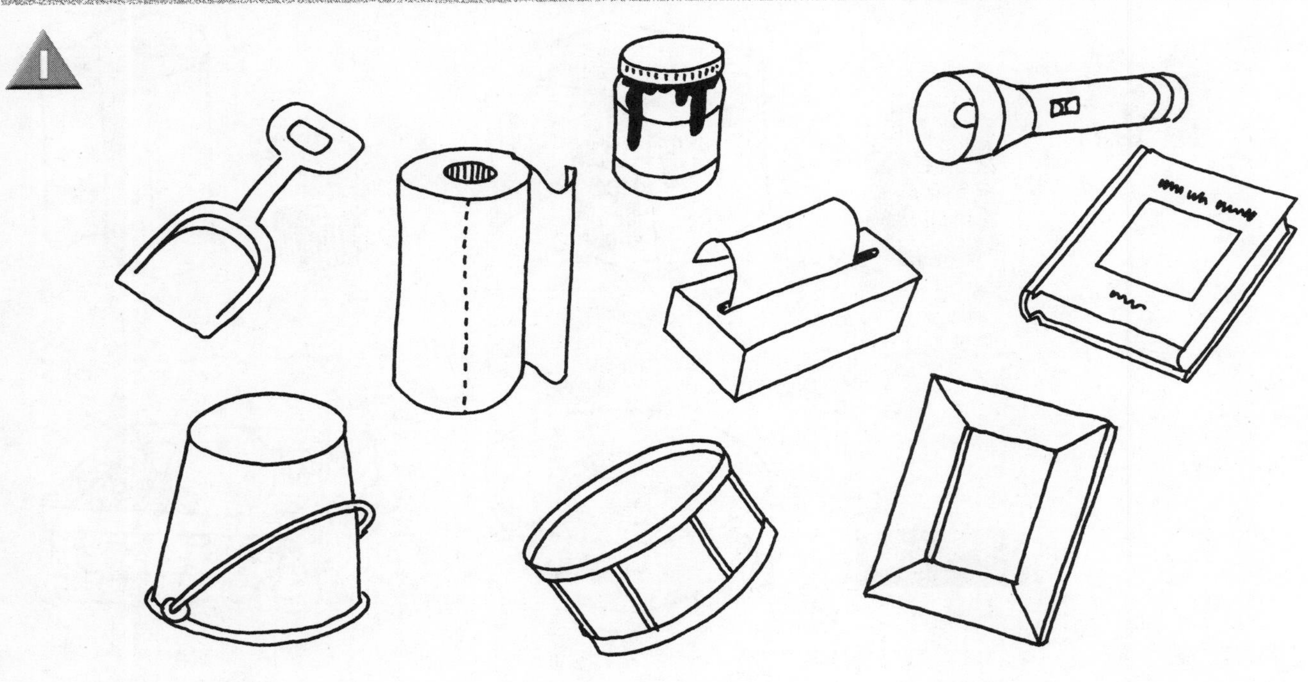

2

Directions: **1** Circle the shapes that have a circular surface. **2** Circle the shapes that have a square surface.

Copyright © Houghton Mifflin Company. All rights reserved.

Name ___________________________

Practice 6.5

Combine Solid Shapes

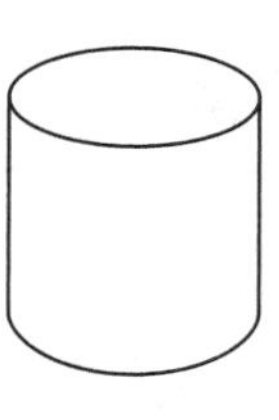

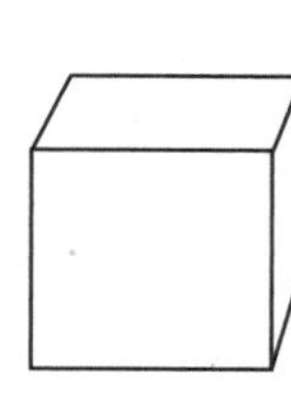

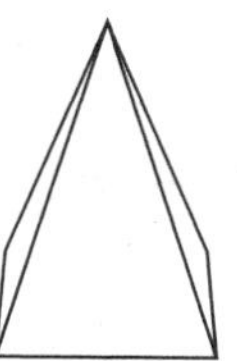

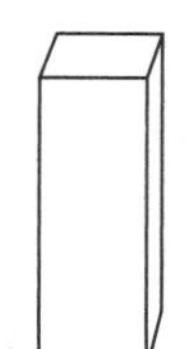

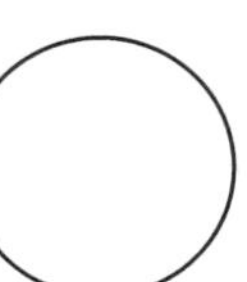

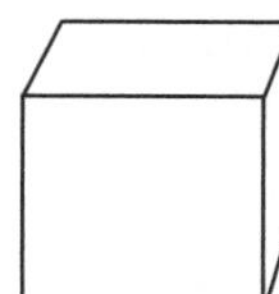

2

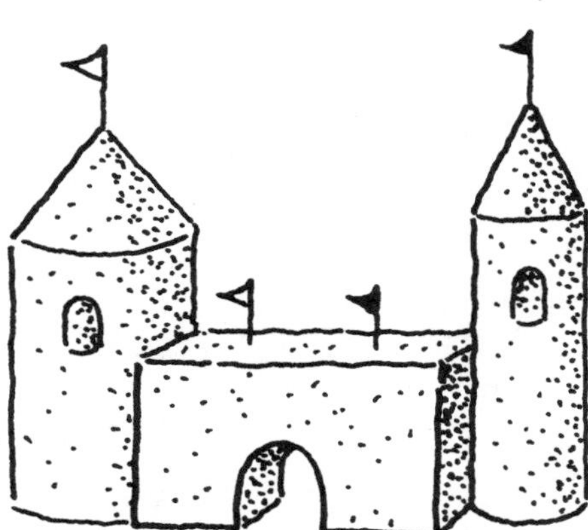

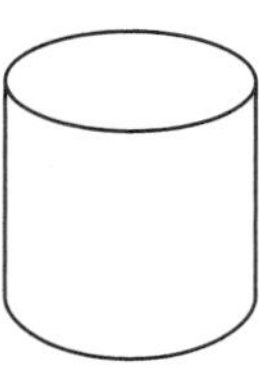

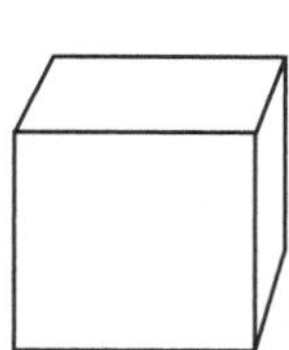

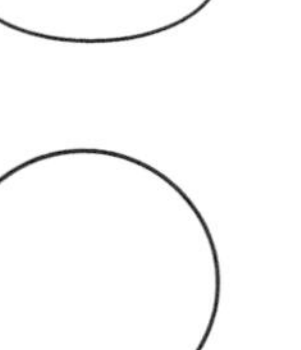

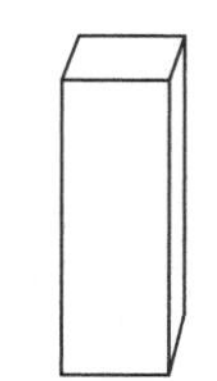

Directions: **1** Color the shapes that were used to make the Jack-in-the-box. **2** Color the shapes that were used to make the sandcastle.

Copyright © Houghton Mifflin Company. All rights reserved.

Name ________________________

Practice 6.6

Problem Solving: Make a Graph

How Many Shapes?

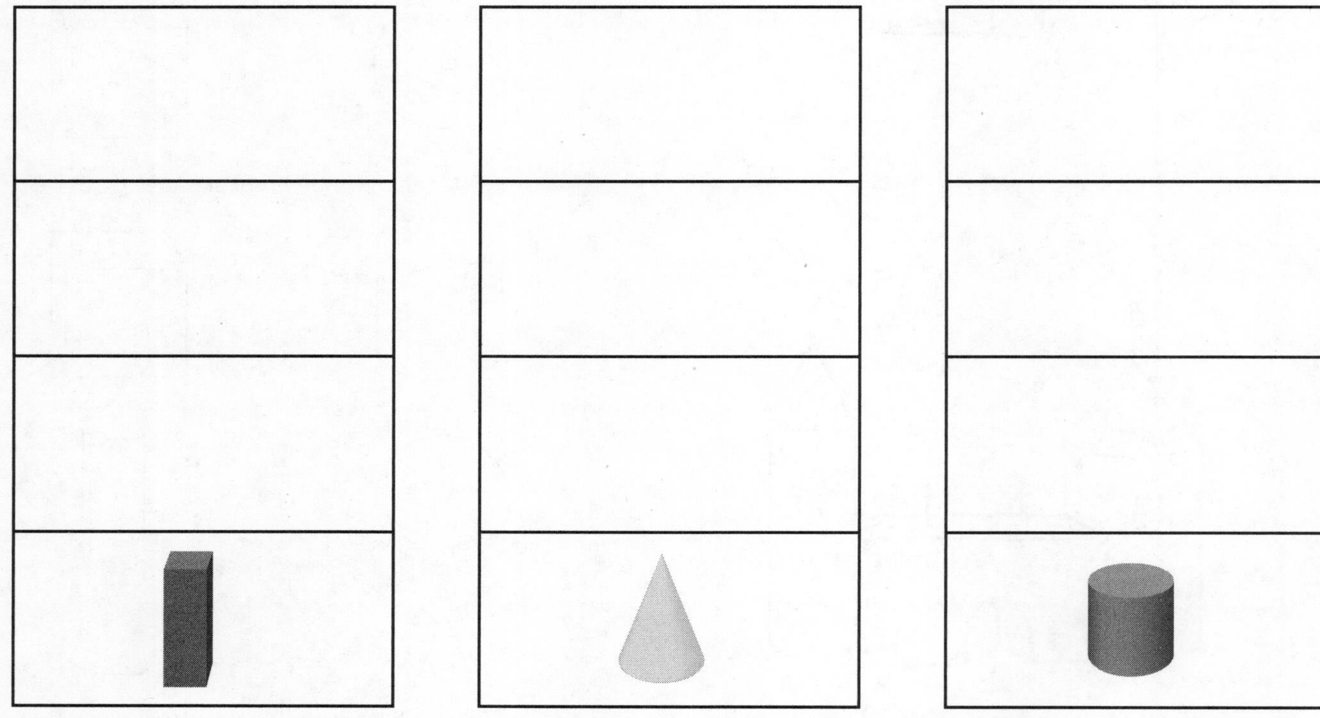

2 ______ ______ ______

Directions: **1** Color one box in the graph for each shape. **2** Count the colored boxes and write the numbers. Compare the numbers of shapes.

Copyright © Houghton Mifflin Company. All rights reserved.

Name ______________________

Practice 7.1

Six

1

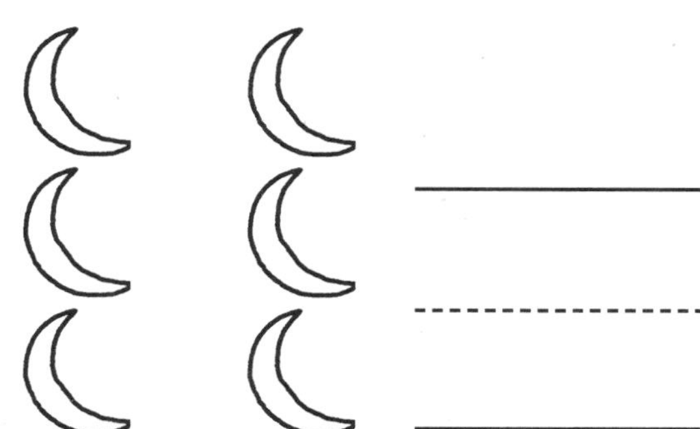

2

3

4

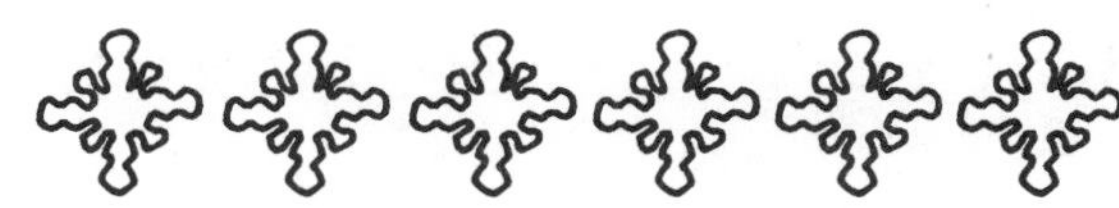

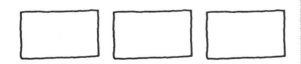

Directions: 1–4 Circle the sets of 6. Write the number.

Copyright © Houghton Mifflin Company. All rights reserved.

Name ____________________

Seven

2    

3     

Directions: 1–4 Count the items. Draw more to make a set of 7. Write the number.

Copyright © Houghton Mifflin Company. All rights reserved.

Name ______________________________

Practice 7.3

Eight

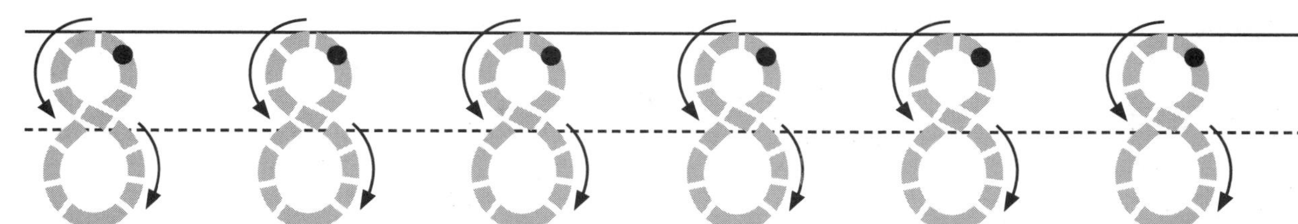

Directions: **I** Circle the groups of 8. **2** Write the number.

Copyright © Houghton Mifflin Company. All rights reserved.

Name ______________________

Nine

1

2

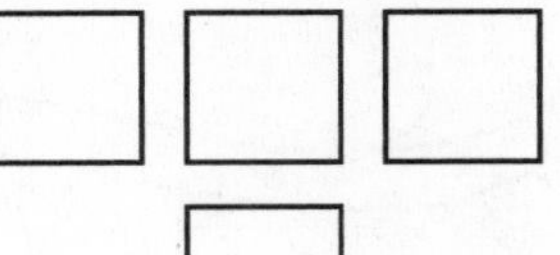

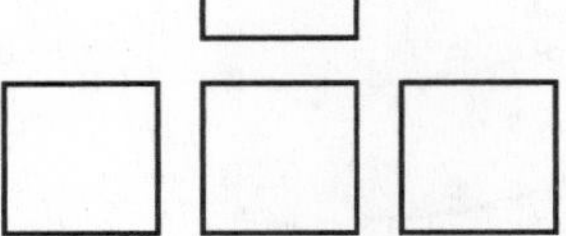

3

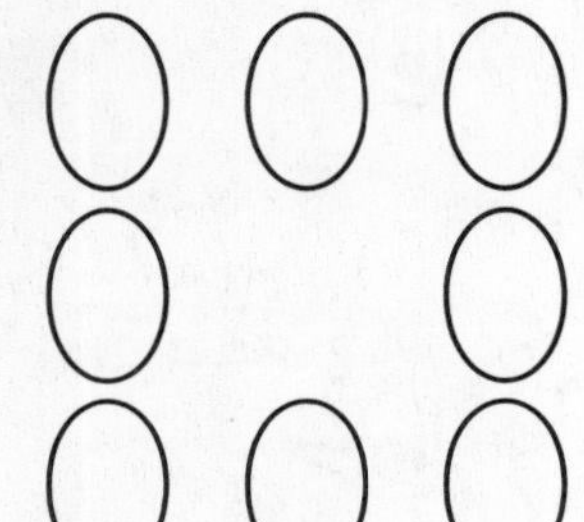

4

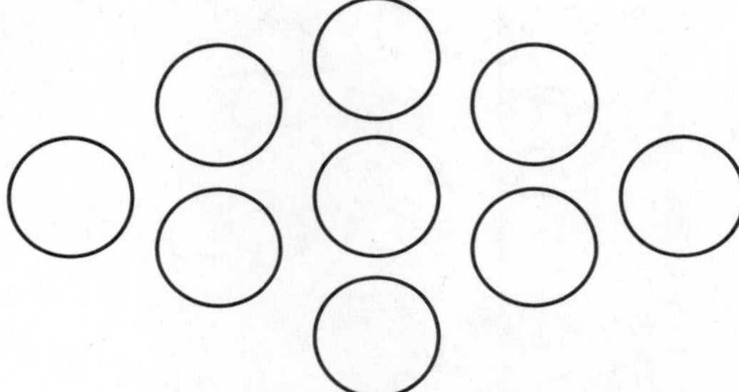

5

Directions: 1–5 Count the items. Write the number.

Copyright © Houghton Mifflin Company. All rights reserved.

Name ______________________

Practice 7.5

Ten

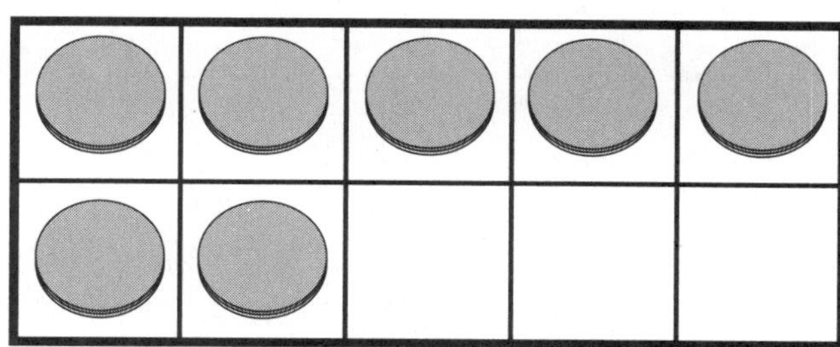

2

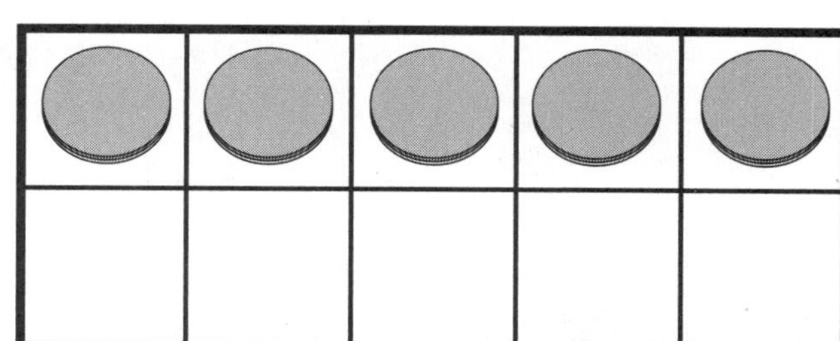

3

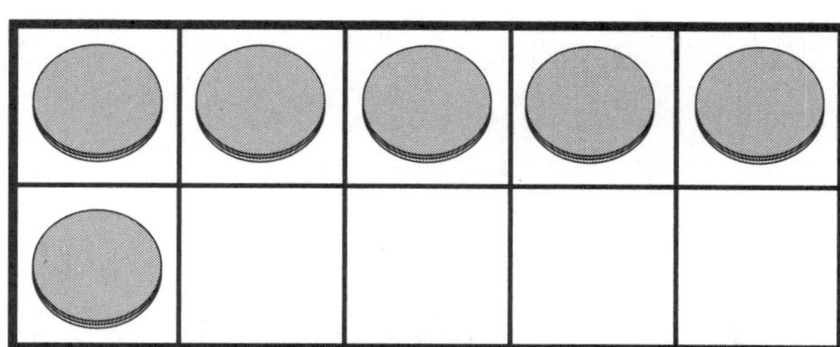

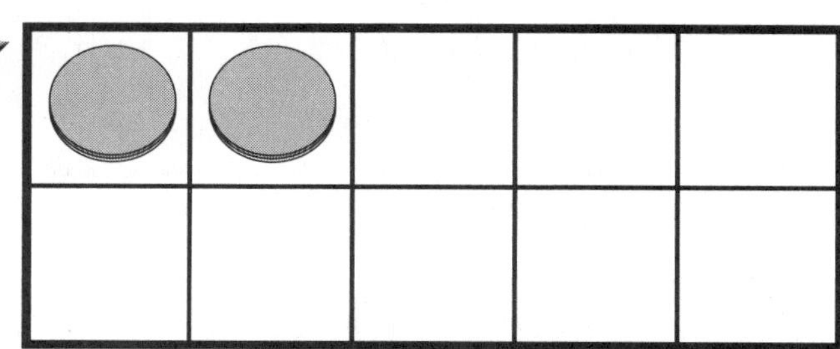

Directions: 1–4 Place counters in the ten-frame to make 10. Draw. Write the number.

Copyright © Houghton Mifflin Company. All rights reserved.

Name ____________________

Practice 7.6

Problem Solving: Use a Pattern

1

2 3 4 5 ____ ____

2

8 7 6 5 ____ ____

3

9 7 5 ____ 1

4

2 4 ____ 8 ____

Directions: 1–4 Count the dots. Look for a pattern. Write the missing number.

Copyright © Houghton Mifflin Company. All rights reserved.

Name ___________________________

Practice 7.7

Eleven

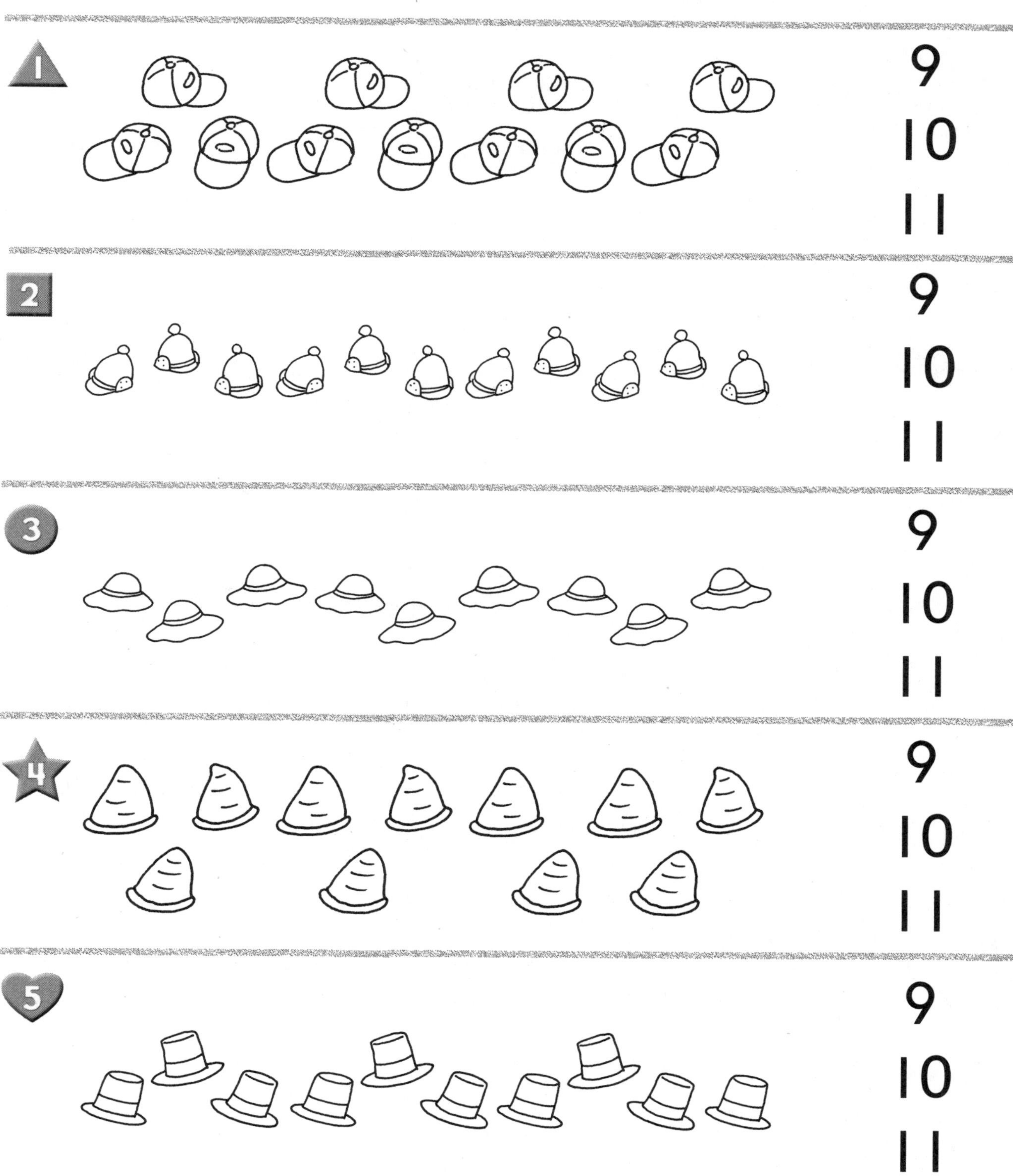

Directions: 1–5 Count the items. Circle the number.

Copyright © Houghton Mifflin Company. All rights reserved.

Name ______________________

Twelve

1

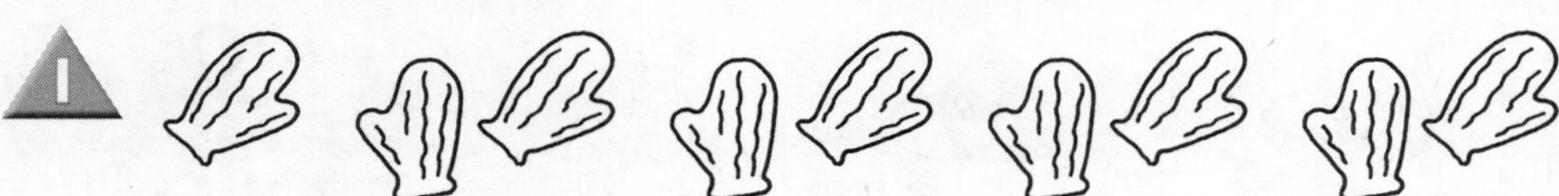

2

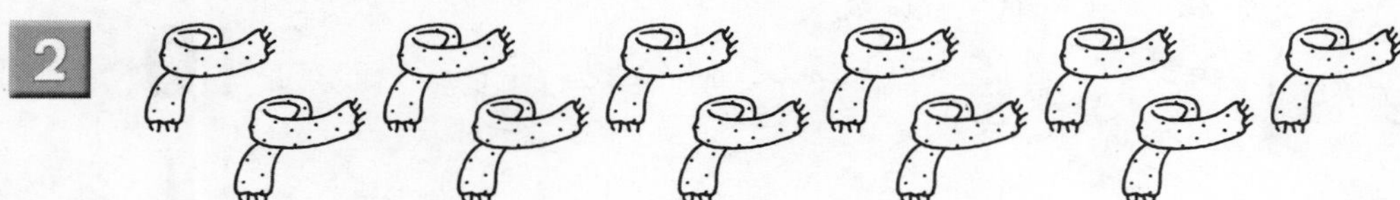

3

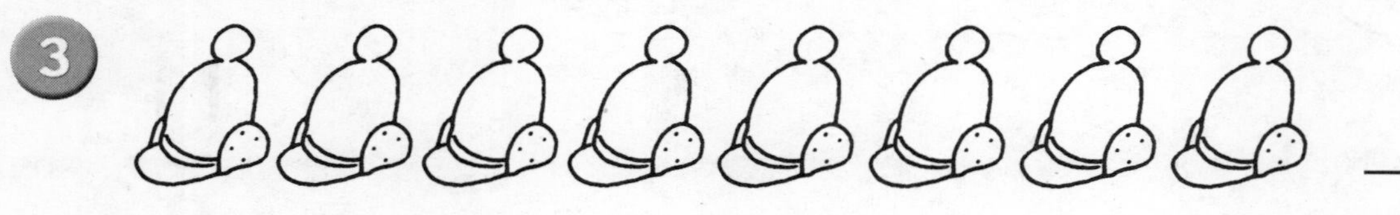

4

Directions: 1–4 Count the objects. Draw more to make 12. Write the number.

Copyright © Houghton Mifflin Company. All rights reserved.

Name ______________________

Practice 8.1

Names for 1–12

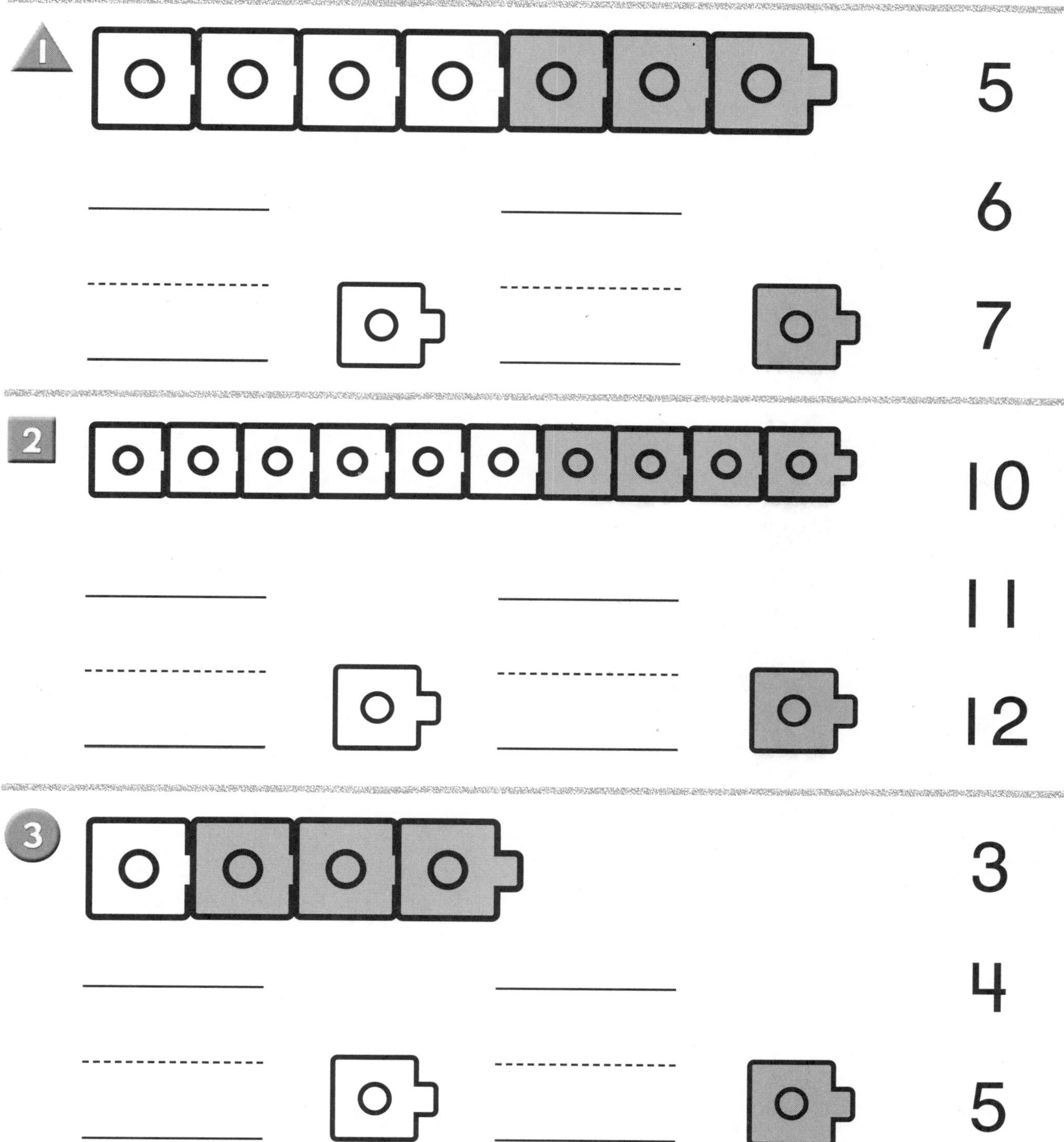

Directions: **1–3** Build the cube train. Count the cubes. Circle the number. Count the cubes of each color. Write the numbers.

Copyright © Houghton Mifflin Company. All rights reserved.

Name ______________________________

Order Numbers to 12

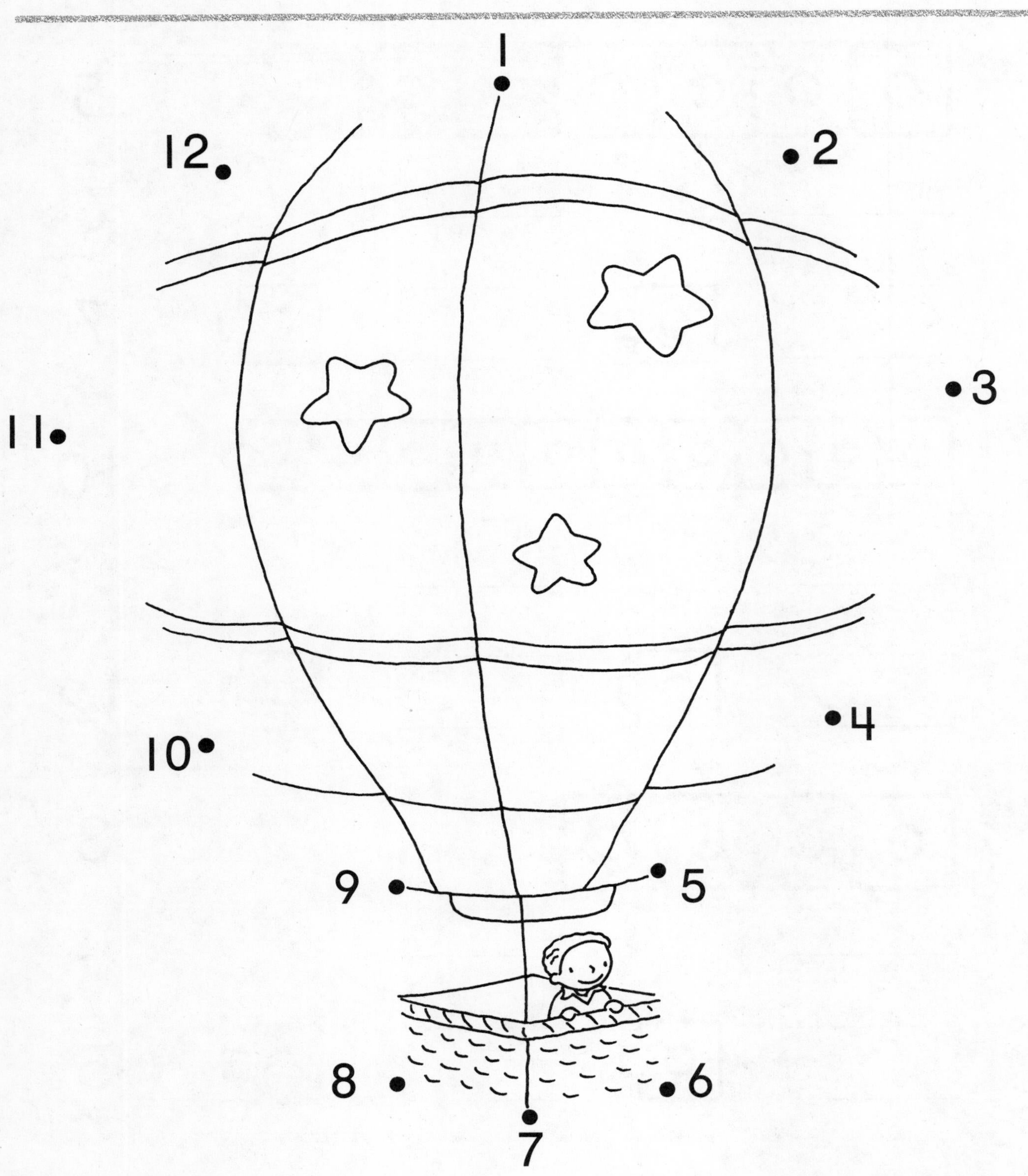

Directions: Connect the dots to make a picture. Color the picture.

Copyright © Houghton Mifflin Company. All rights reserved.

Name ______________________________

Sort by Number

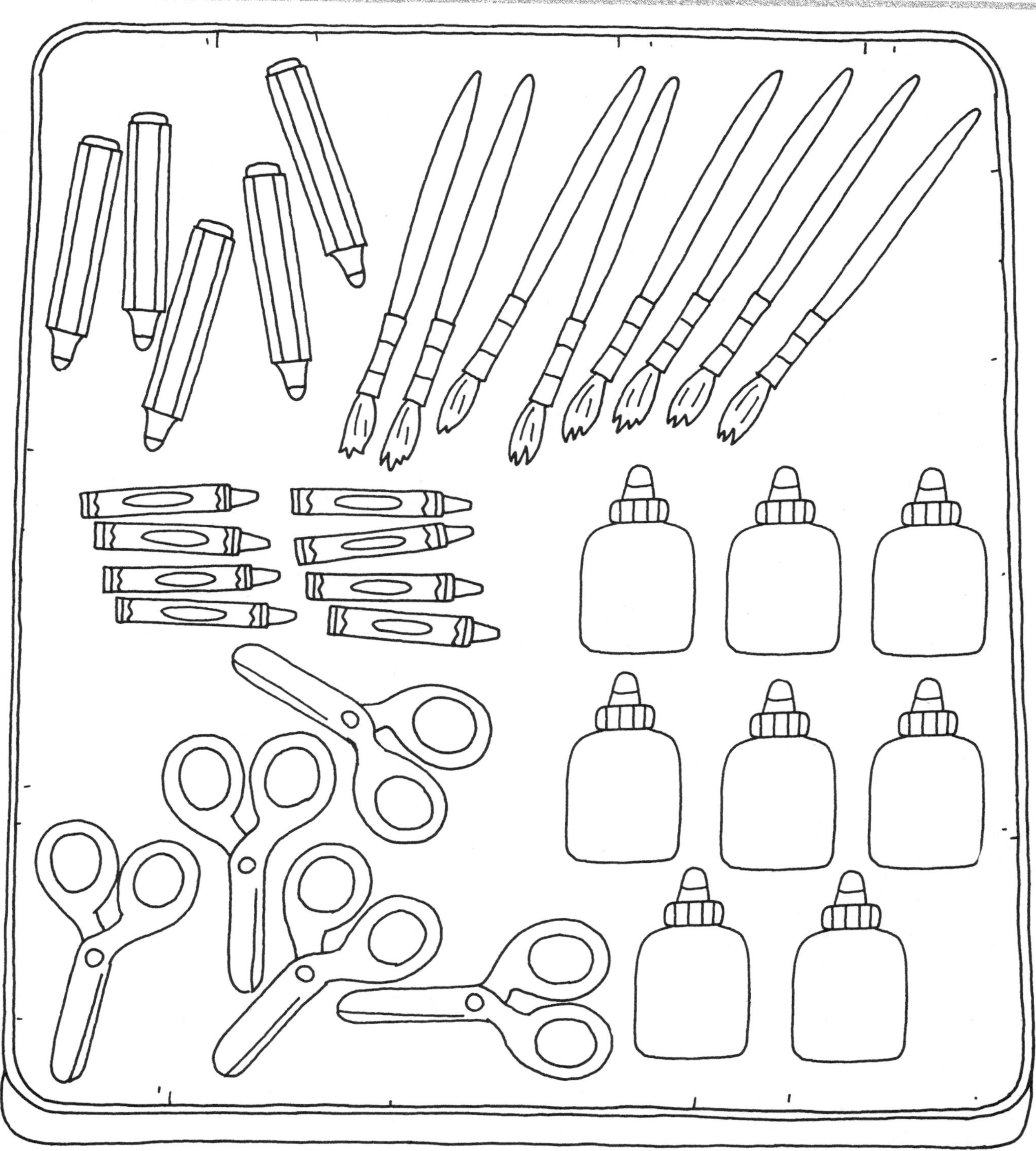

Directions: Circle sets of 5 blue. Circle sets of 8 red.

Copyright © Houghton Mifflin Company. All rights reserved.

Name ______________________

Practice 8.4

More and Fewer

1

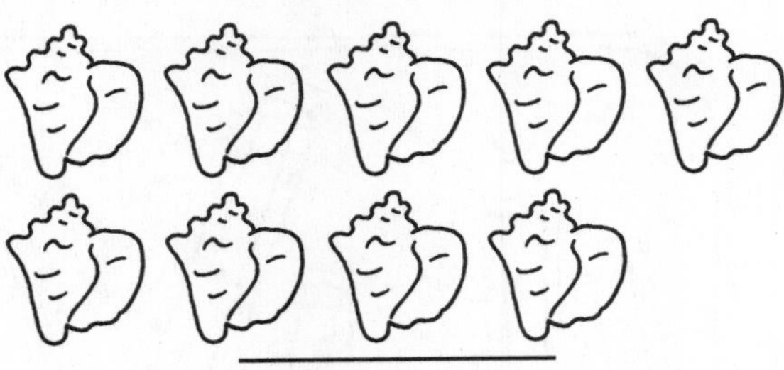

2

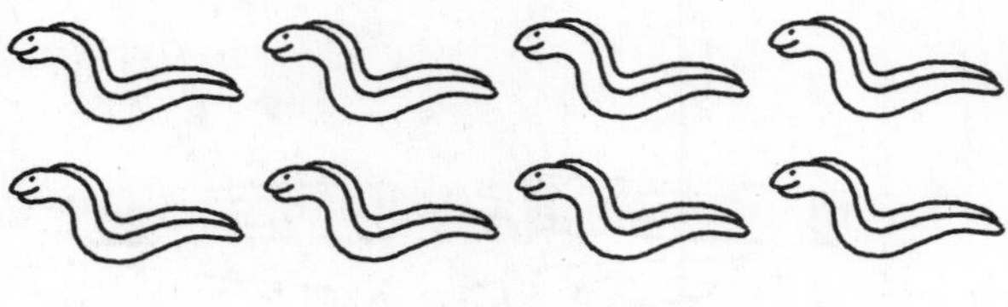

3

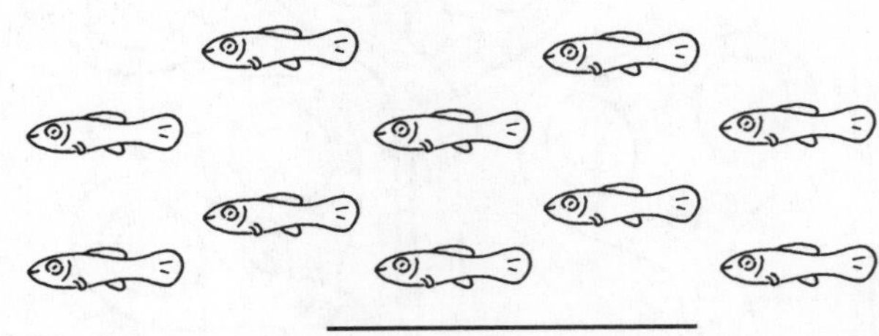

Directions: **1–3** Count. Tell which set has more and which has fewer. Write each number. Circle the greater number.

Copyright © Houghton Mifflin Company. All rights reserved.

Name ____________________

Practice 8.5

Estimate Quantities

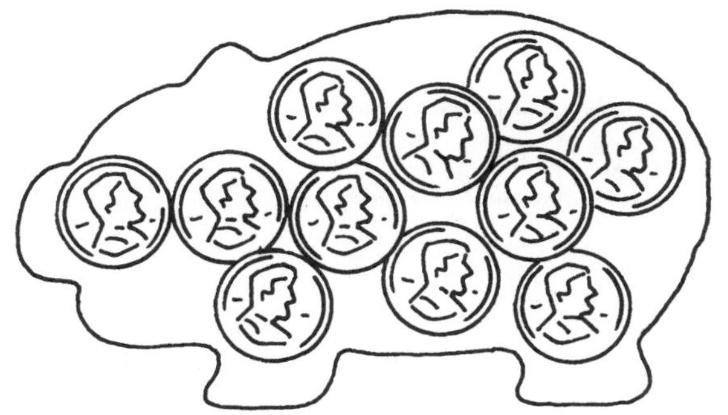

Estimate	Count

2

Estimate	Count

3

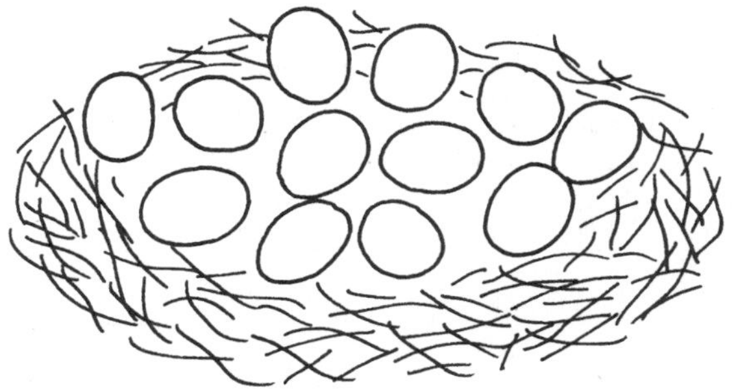

Estimate	Count

Estimate	Count

Directions: 1–4 Estimate the number in each set. Write the number. Then count the items. Write how many.

Copyright © Houghton Mifflin Company. All rights reserved.

Name ______________________

Practice 8.6

Problem Solving: Act It Out

2

3

4

Directions: Build the cube train. Break it into equal groups to show: **1** groups of 2 cubes; **2** groups of three cubes; **3** groups of four cubes; **4** groups of six cubes. Draw lines to show where you broke each train. Write the number of equal groups you made.

Copyright © Houghton Mifflin Company. All rights reserved.

Name ______________________________

Practice 9.1

Times of Day

2

3

Directions: Circle the picture that shows: **1** the morning; **2** the afternoon; **3** the evening.

Copyright © Houghton Mifflin Company. All rights reserved.

Name ______________________

Practice 9.2

Days and Months on the Calendar

1

Wednesday	Thursday	Friday	Saturday Sunday

2

Saturday	Sunday	Monday	Wednesday Tuesday

3

September	October	November	January December

4

January	February	March	April May

5

May	June	July	September August

Directions: 1–2 Circle the day that comes next. **3–5** Circle the month that comes next.

Copyright © Houghton Mifflin Company. All rights reserved.

Name ________________________________

Practice 9.3

Comparing Temperature

2

3

Directions: **1–3** Color a red frame around the picture that shows a hotter day. Color a blue frame around the picture that shows a colder day.

Copyright © Houghton Mifflin Company. All rights reserved.

Name ______________________

Practice 9.4

Problem-Solving: Use a Picture

May						
Sunday	Monday	Tuesday	Wednesday	Thursday	Friday	Saturday
				1	2	3
4	5	6	7	8	9	10
11	12	13	14	15	16	17
18	19	20	21	22	23	24
25	26	27	28	29	30	31

1 ______ Saturdays

2 ______ Thursdays

3 ______ Fridays

4 ______ Wednesdays

Directions: Count and write the number of: **1** Saturdays; **2** Thursdays; **3** Fridays; **4** Wednesdays. Circle the first Tuesday in blue, the last Monday in red, and all the Sundays in green.

Copyright © Houghton Mifflin Company. All rights reserved.

Name ______________________

More Time, Less Time

2

3

Directions: 1–3 Circle in red the activity that takes more time. Circle in blue the activity that takes less time.

Copyright © Houghton Mifflin Company. All rights reserved.

Name ________________________________

Practice 9.6

Order Events

2

3

Directions: 1–3 Write the numbers *1, 2,* and *3* to show the order of events from first to last.

Copyright © Houghton Mifflin Company. All rights reserved.

Name ______________________

Practice 9.7

Time to the Hour

______

______ o'clock

2

______

______ o'clock

3

______

______ o'clock

______

______ o'clock

______

______ o'clock

Directions: 1–5 Write the time shown on the clock.

Copyright © Houghton Mifflin Company. All rights reserved.

Name ______________________

Practice 9.8

More Time to the Hour

1 3:00

______ o'clock

2 9:00

______ o'clock

3 

______ o'clock

4 

______ o'clock

5 

______ o'clock

Directions: 1–5 Write the time shown on the clock.

Copyright © Houghton Mifflin Company. All rights reserved.

Name ______________________________

Practice 9.9

Compare Digital and Analog Clocks

2

3

Directions: 1–5 Write the time shown on the clock.

Copyright © Houghton Mifflin Company. All rights reserved.

Use with Teacher's Edition pages 179A–180.

Name ______________________________

Practice 10.1

Sort and Graph Coins

Directions: Count each kind of coin at the top of the page. Color the boxes to show how many.

Copyright © Houghton Mifflin Company. All rights reserved.

Use with Teacher's Edition pages 184A–184D.

Name ___________________________

Practice 10.2

Penny

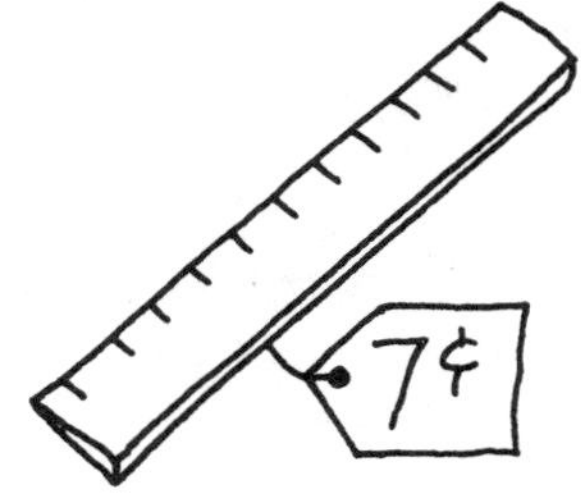

Directions: 1–5 Use pennies to show each price. Draw the pennies.

Copyright © Houghton Mifflin Company. All rights reserved.

Name ______________________________

Nickel

1

2

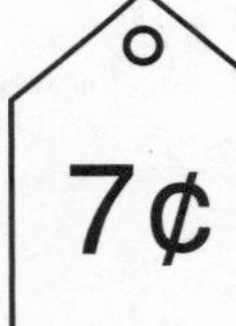

4

10¢ 11¢

Directions: 1–4 Circle the price tag that matches the number of cents.

Copyright © Houghton Mifflin Company. All rights reserved.

Name ___________________________________

Practice 10.4

Dime

10¢ 5¢ 1¢

2

9¢ 10¢ 11¢

9¢ 10¢ 11¢

4

12¢ 11¢ 10¢

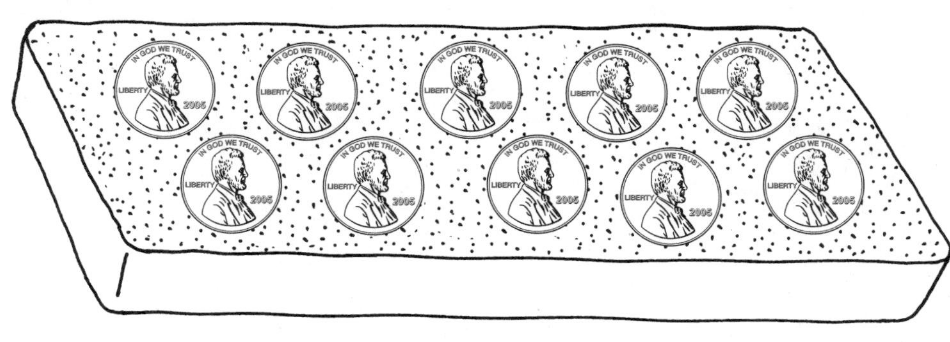

9¢ 10¢ 11¢

Directions: 1–5 Circle the number of cents.

Copyright © Houghton Mifflin Company. All rights reserved.

Name ______________________

Practice 10.5

Quarter

Directions: Circle all the quarters. Count and write the number of quarters.

Copyright © Houghton Mifflin Company. All rights reserved.

Name ______________________

Practice 10.6

Problem Solving: Act It Out

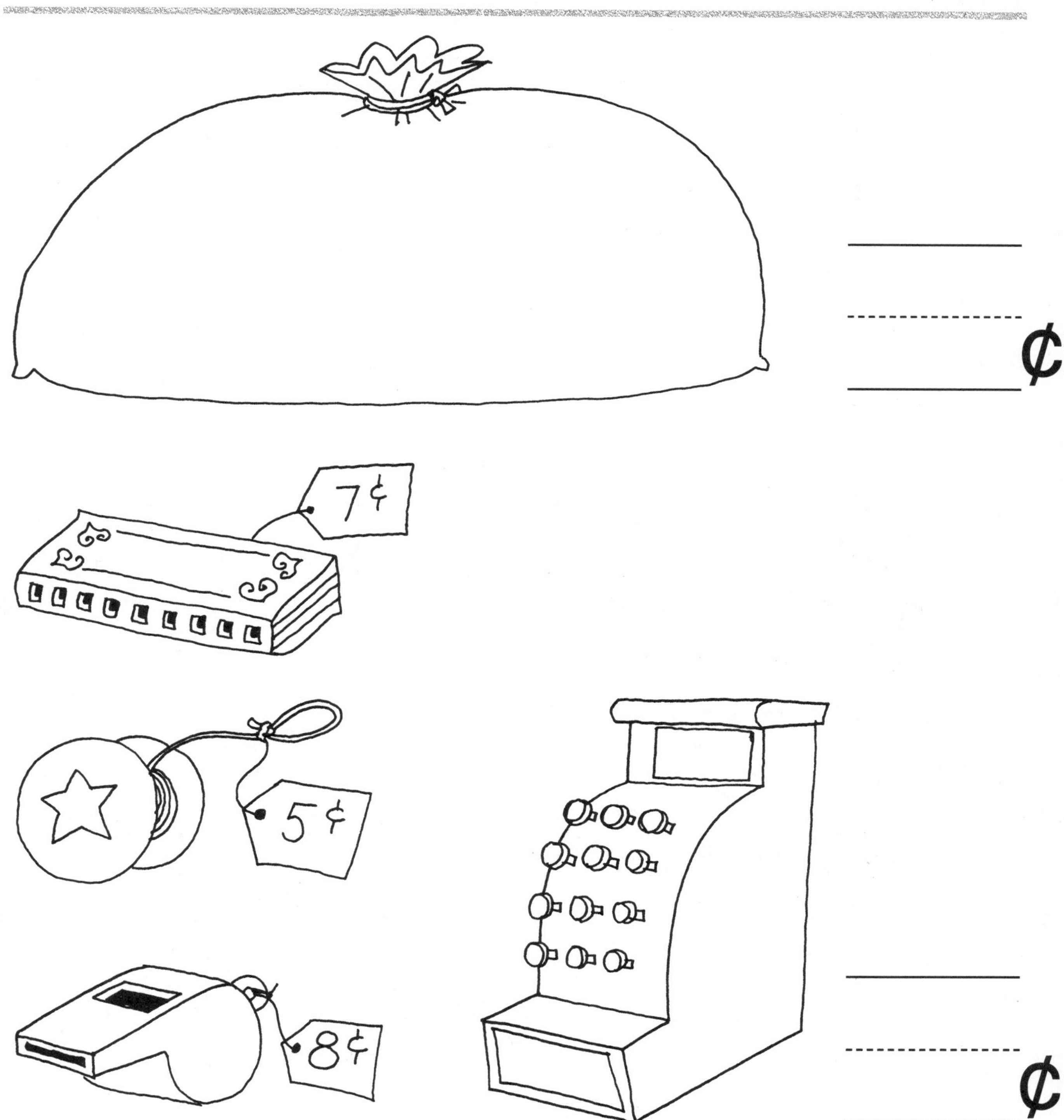

Directions: Place 10 pennies on the purse. Circle an item you want to buy. Move that many cents to the cash register. Write how much you spent. Write what you have left in the purse.

Copyright © Houghton Mifflin Company. All rights reserved.

Name ______________________________

Practice 11.1

Compare Length

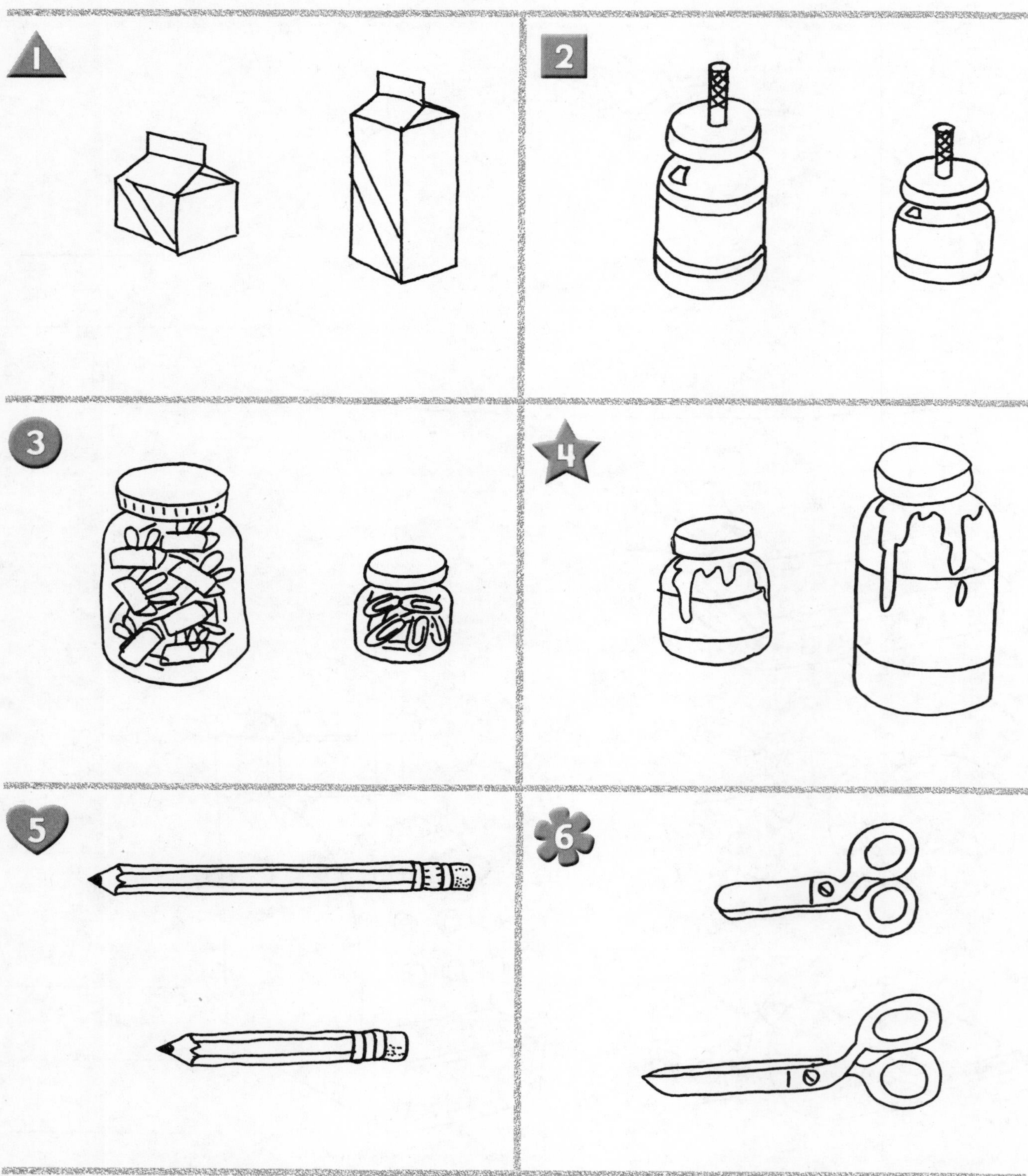

Directions: **1–4** Circle the taller one. Underline the shorter one. **5–6** Circle the longer one. Underline the shorter one.

Copyright © Houghton Mifflin Company. All rights reserved.

Use with Teacher's Edition pages 205A–206.

Name ______________________

Practice 11.2

Order by Length

Directions: **1–4** Write the numbers *1, 2,* and *3* to order the items from shortest to tallest.
5 Write the numbers *1, 2,* and *3* to order the items from shortest to longest.

Copyright © Houghton Mifflin Company. All rights reserved.

Name ____________________

Practice 11.3

Measure Length

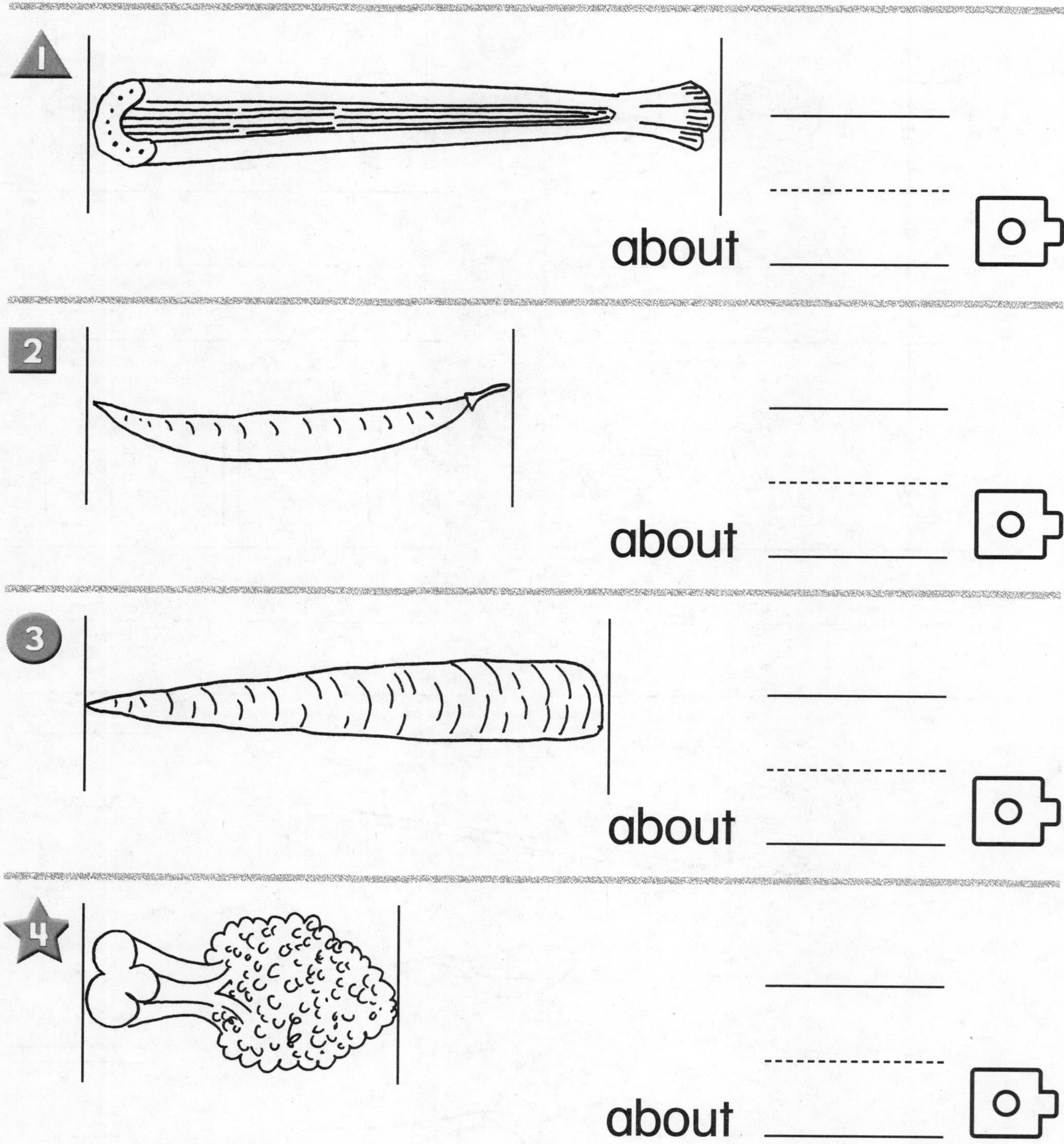

Directions: 1–4 Use cubes to measure the length. Record the length.

Copyright © Houghton Mifflin Company. All rights reserved.

Name ______________________

Practice 11.4

Estimate and Measure Length

1 

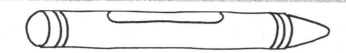

Estimate	Measure
about ______ 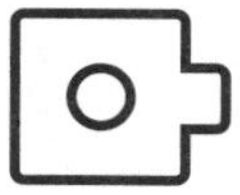	about ______ 

2 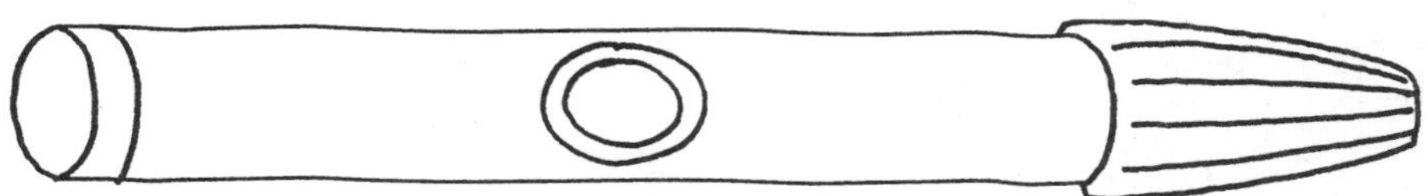

Estimate	Measure
about ______ 	about ______ 

3

Estimate	Measure
about ______ 	about ______ 

Directions: 1–3 Estimate how many cubes long. Measure. Record the length. Compare the measurement to the estimate.

Copyright © Houghton Mifflin Company. All rights reserved.

Name ______________________

Explore Area

1

2

3

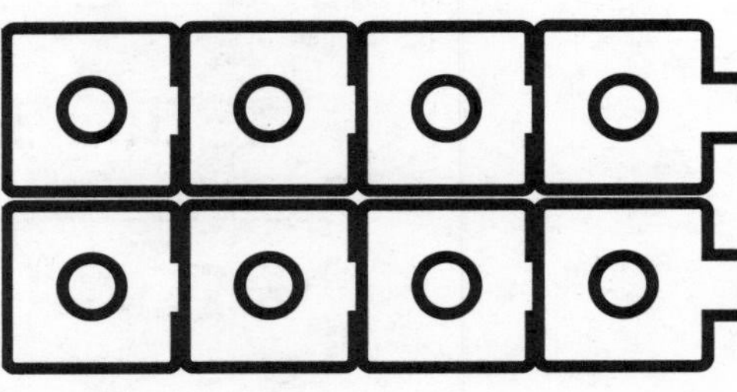

5

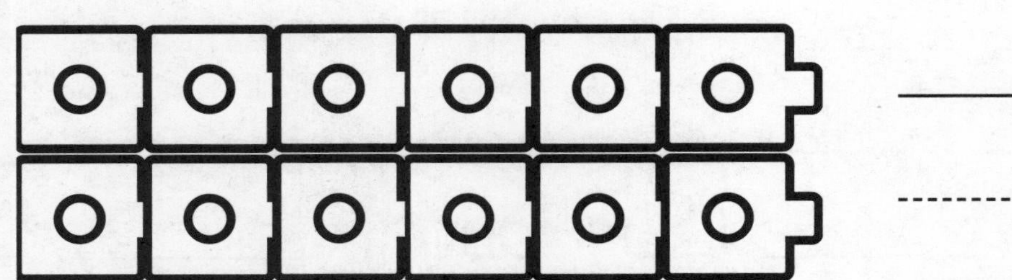

Directions: 1–5 Find the area in cube units. Record the area.

Copyright © Houghton Mifflin Company. All rights reserved.

Name ______________________________

Practice 11.6

Problem Solving: Act It Out

Estimate ________ ----------------

about ________ 

Measure ________ ----------------

about ________ 

2

Estimate ________ ----------------

about ________ 

Measure ________ ----------------

about ________ 

3

Estimate ________ ----------------

about ________

Measure ________ ----------------

about ________ 

Directions: Estimate the number of: **1** hands tall the chair is; **2** foot lengths long the rug is; **3** forearms the bookshelf is. Measure and record. Compare measurements to estimates.

Copyright © Houghton Mifflin Company. All rights reserved.

Name ______________________________

Practice 12.1

Compare Weight

2

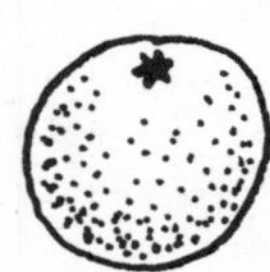

3

5

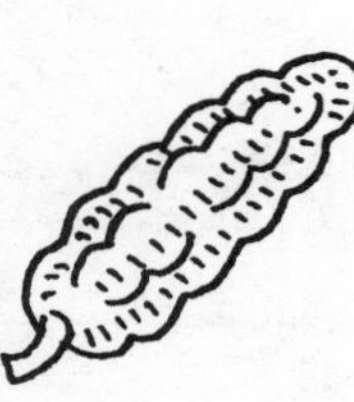

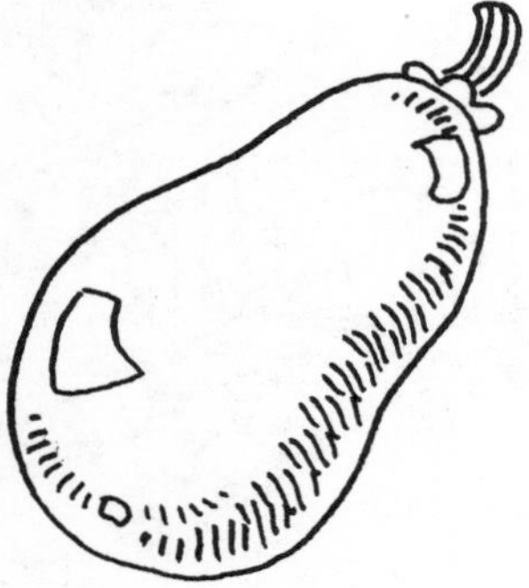

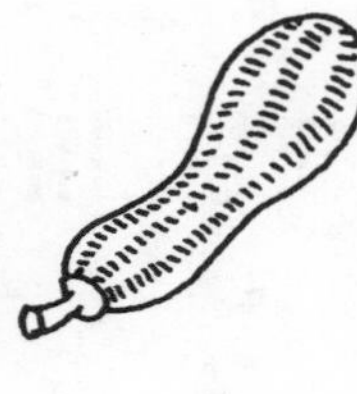

Directions: **1–4** Circle the heavier one. Underline the lighter one. **5** Circle the two that are about the same weight.

Copyright © Houghton Mifflin Company. All rights reserved.

Name ____________________

Practice 12.2

Order by Weight

2

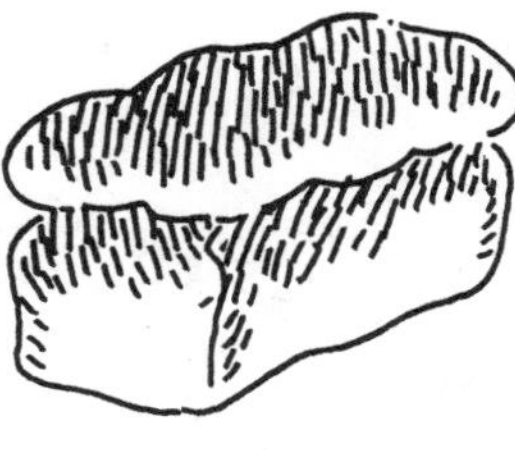

Directions: 1–3 Write the numbers *1, 2,* and *3* to order the items from lightest to heaviest.

Copyright © Houghton Mifflin Company. All rights reserved.

Name ____________________

Practice 12.3

Measure Weight

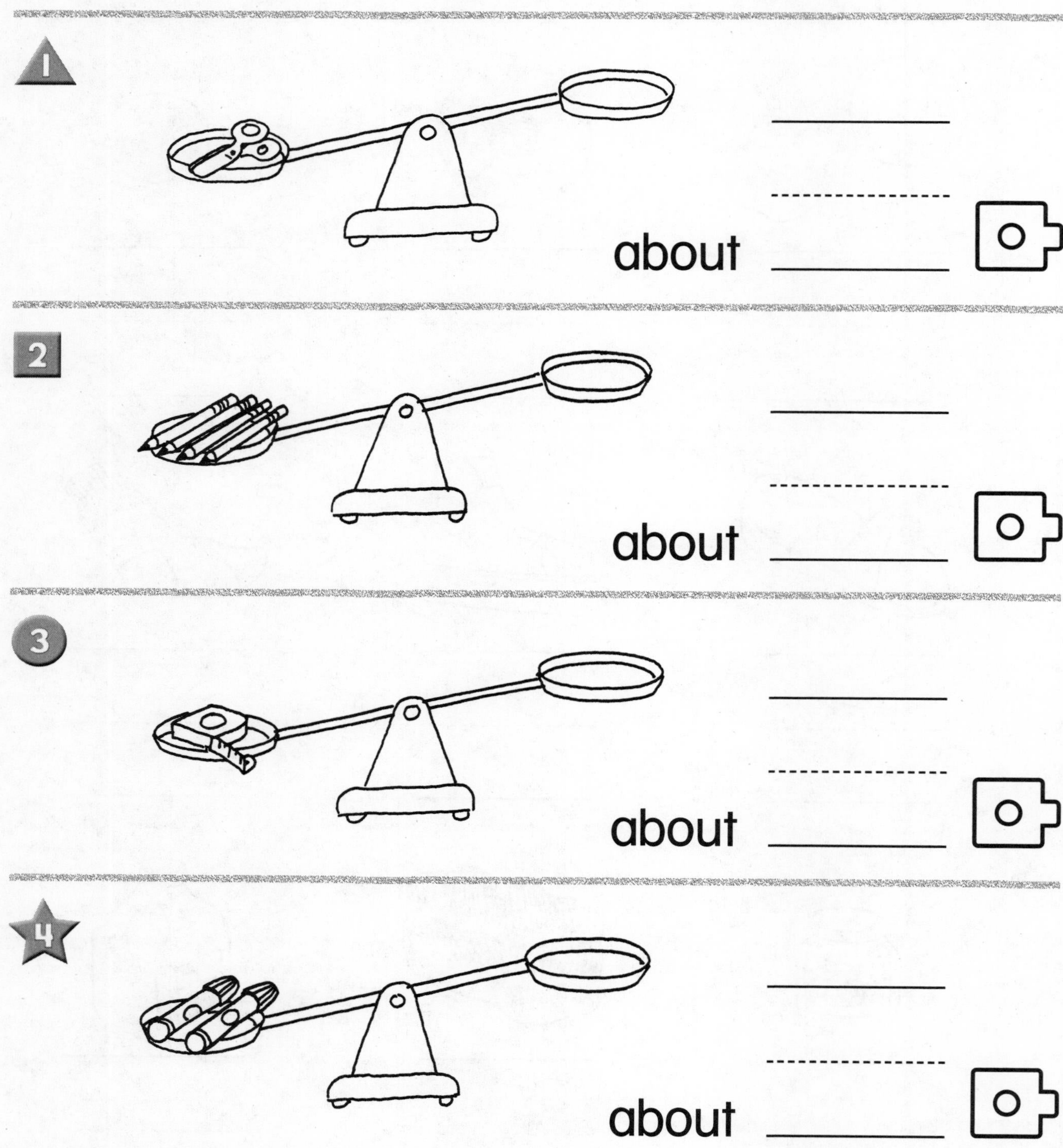

Directions: 1–4 Use cubes to measure objects like the ones shown. Record the weight.

Copyright © Houghton Mifflin Company. All rights reserved.

Use with Teacher's Edition pages 222A–222D.

Name ______________________

Practice 12.4

Estimate and Measure Weight

1 Estimate ________ Measure ________

about ________ [cube] about ________ [cube]

2 Estimate ________ Measure ________

about ________ [cube] about ________ [cube]

3 Estimate ________ Measure ________

about ________ [cube] about ________ [cube]

4 Estimate ________ Measure ________

about ________ [cube] about ________ [cube]

Directions: 1–4 Use an object like the one shown. Estimate how many cubes are needed to balance the buckets. Measure. Record the number of cubes. Compare the measurement to the estimate.

Copyright © Houghton Mifflin Company. All rights reserved.

Name ______________________

Practice 12.5

Compare Capacity

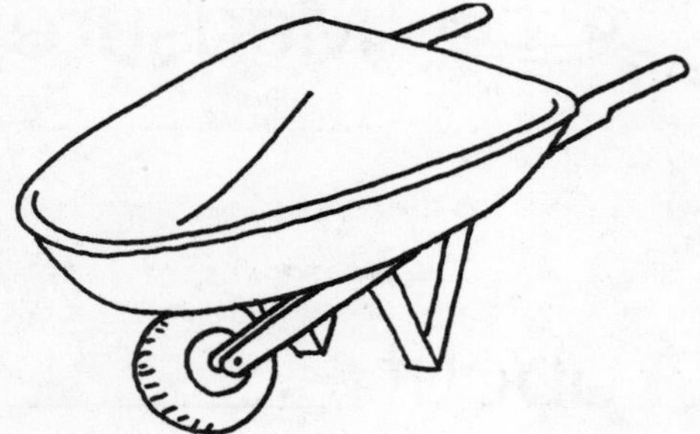

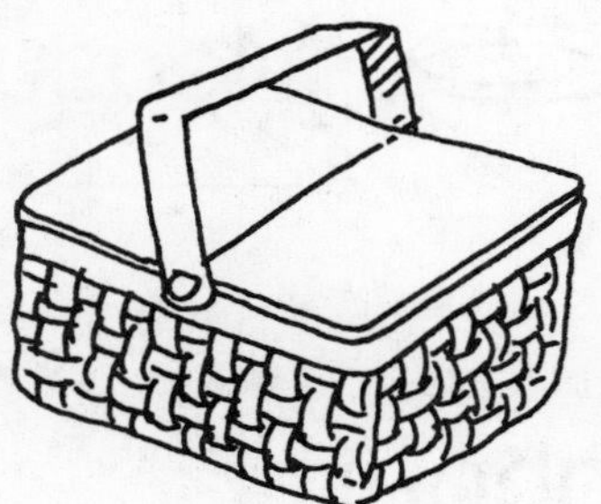

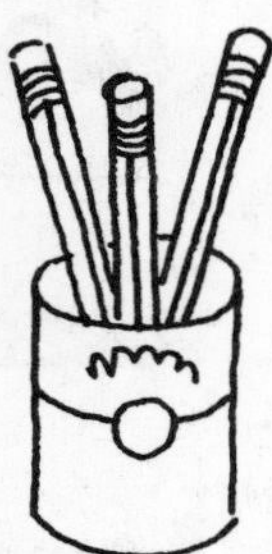

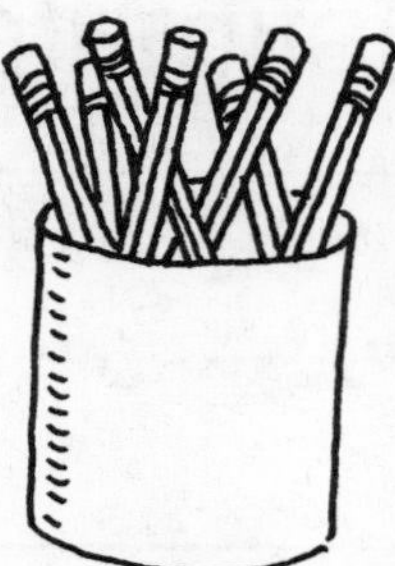

Directions: 1–4 Compare the kinds of containers. Circle the one that holds more. Underline the one that holds less.

Copyright © Houghton Mifflin Company. All rights reserved.

Name ______________________________

Practice 12.6

Order by Capacity

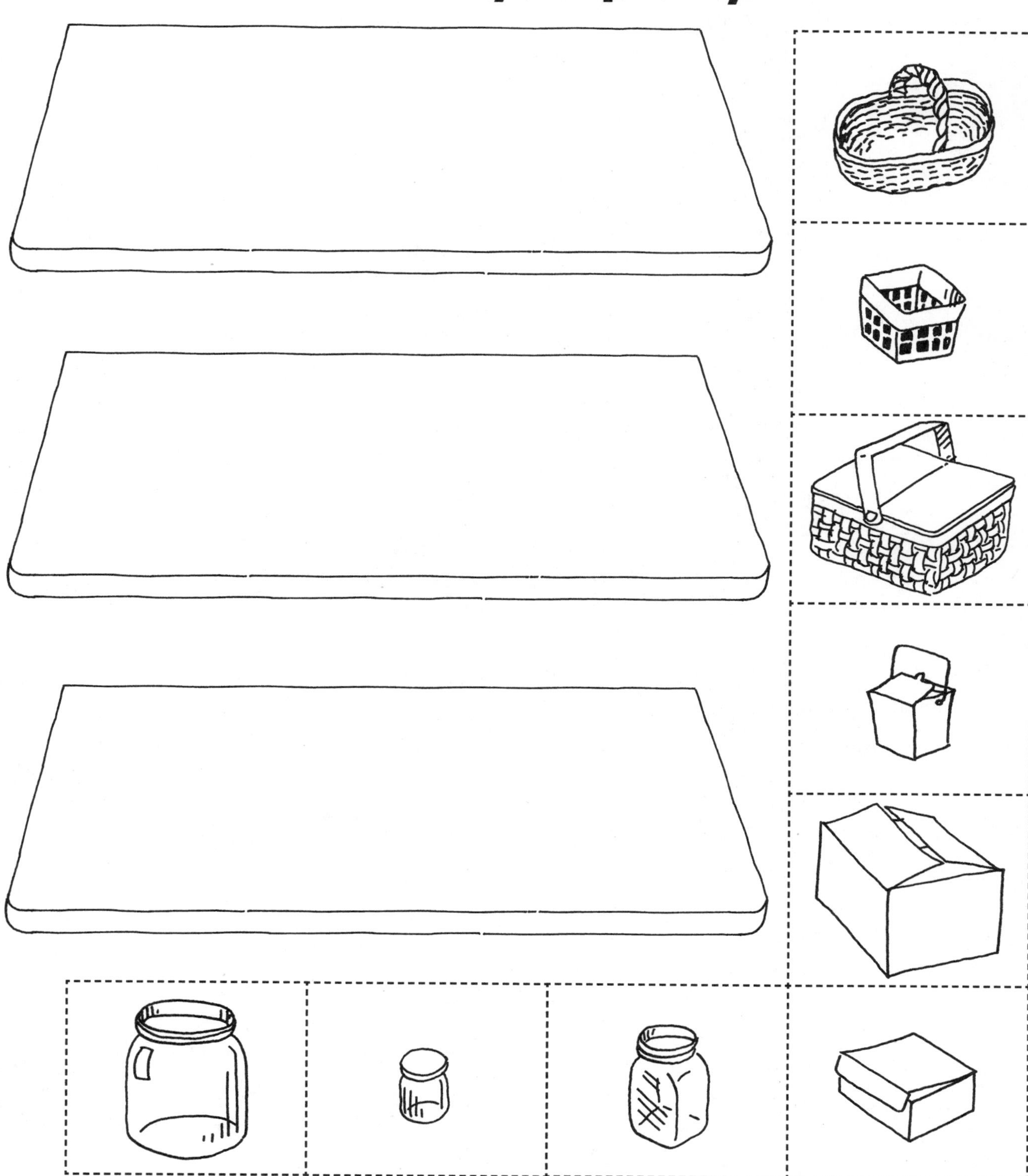

Directions: Cut out the pictures. Sort and glue them on the shelves in order from the one that holds the least to the one that holds the most.

Copyright © Houghton Mifflin Company. All rights reserved.

Use with Teacher's Edition pages 227A–228.

Name ______________________________

Practice 12.7

Measure Capacity

about ________ 

2

about ________ 

3

about ________ 

about ________ 

Directions: **1–4** Use a container like the one shown. Measure to find out how many cups of beans are needed to fill the container. Record the number of cups.

Copyright © Houghton Mifflin Company. All rights reserved.

Name ______________________

Practice 12.8

Estimate and Measure Capacity

1

Estimate ______ about ______

Measure ______ about ______

2

Estimate ______ about ______

Measure ______ about ______

3

Estimate ______ about ______

Measure ______ about ______

4

Estimate ______ about ______

Measure ______ about ______

Directions: 1–4 Use a container like the one shown. Estimate how many cups of beans are needed to fill the container. Measure. Record the number of cups. Compare the measurement to the estimate.

Copyright © Houghton Mifflin Company. All rights reserved.

Name ______________________

Practice 12.9

Tools for Measuring

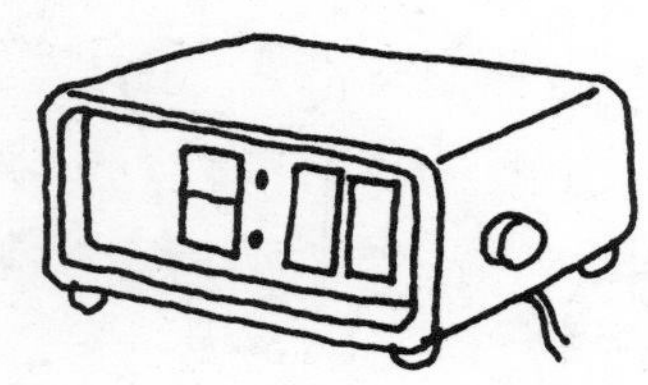

2

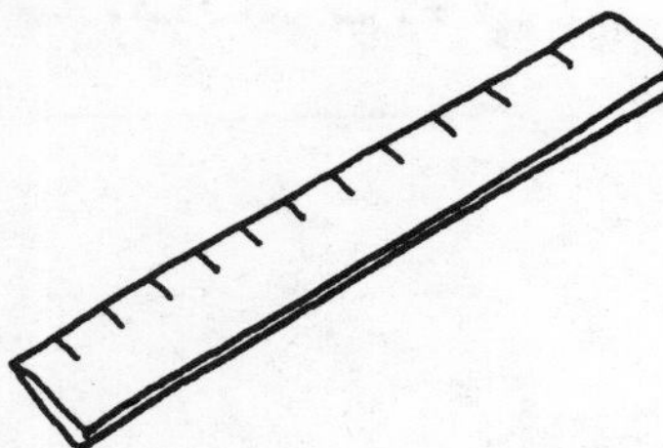

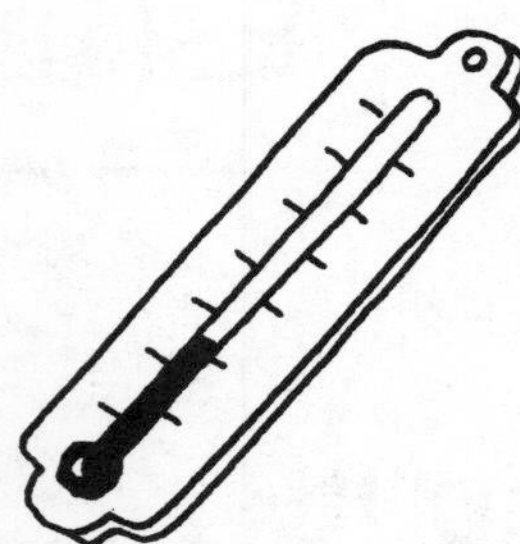

3

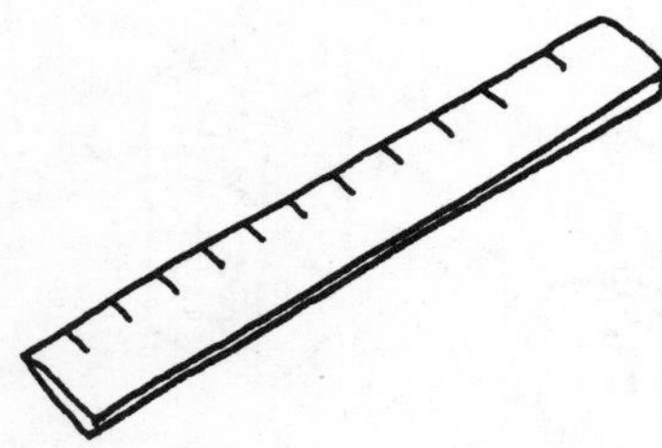

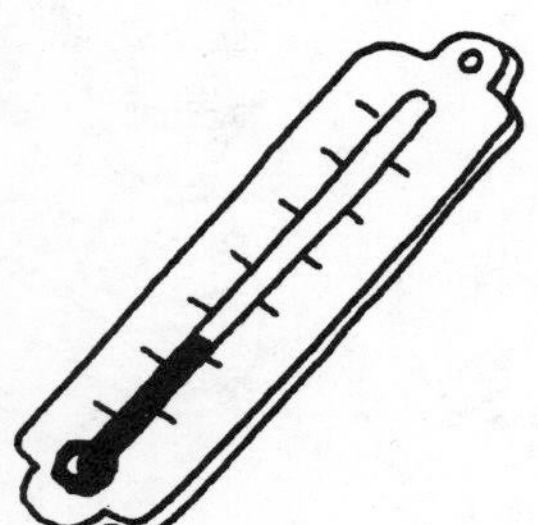

Directions: Circle the tool used to: **1** tell if it is time to go to bed; **2** measure how long a box is; **3** count how many days are left in the month; **4** find out if a pencil and a crayon weigh about the same.

Copyright © Houghton Mifflin Company. All rights reserved.

Name ____________________

Practice 12.10

Problem Solving: Use Logical Reasoning

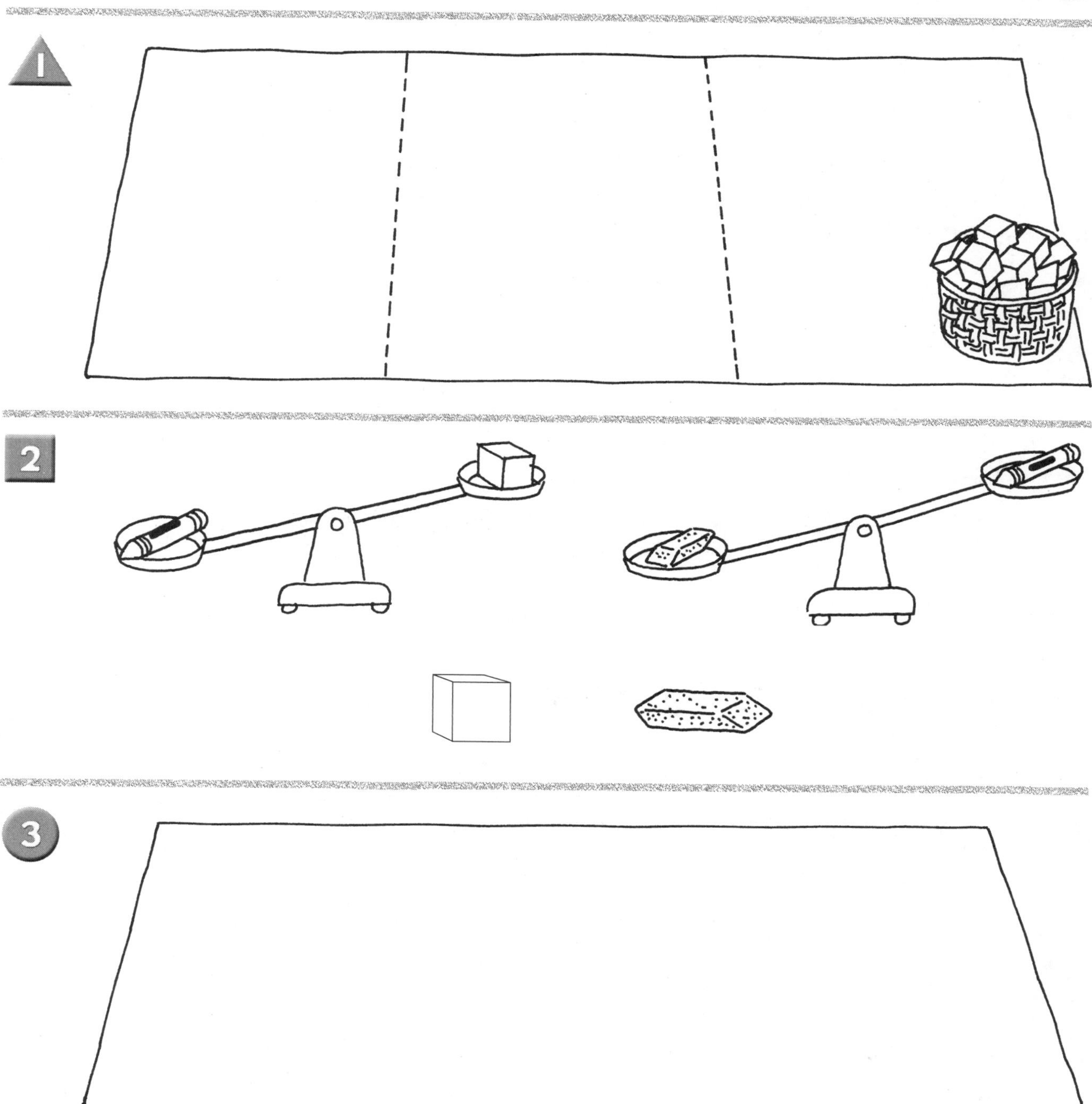

Directions: **1** Draw three block towers. The middle tower is taller than the first tower. The first tower is taller than the last. Circle the tallest tower. **2** Circle the item that is lighter. **3** Draw a blue cup that holds less than a green cup. Draw a red cup that holds less than the blue cup. Circle the cup that holds the most.

Copyright © Houghton Mifflin Company. All rights reserved.

Name ______________________

Practice 13.1

Model Addition

2

3

Directions: 1–4 Tell a story about how the picture shows adding more. Write how many in all.

Copyright © Houghton Mifflin Company. All rights reserved.

Name ______________________

Practice 13.2

Add 1 to Numbers 0–9

Directions: 1–4 Tell a story about how the picture shows adding one. Write how many in all.

Copyright © Houghton Mifflin Company. All rights reserved.

Name ______________________

Practice 13.3

Add 2 to Numbers 0–5

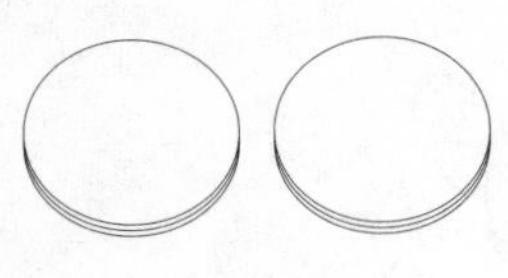

3 + 2 = ____

2

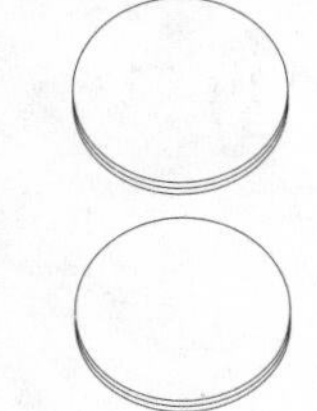

4 + 2 = ____

3

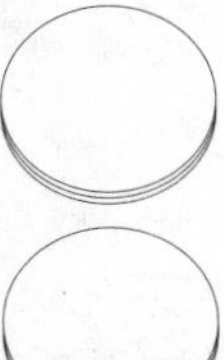

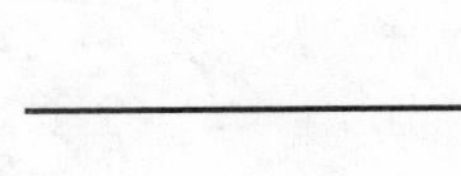

5 + 2 = ____

Directions: 1–3 Show each number with counters. Draw. Write how many in all.

Copyright © Houghton Mifflin Company. All rights reserved.

Use with Teacher's Edition pages 247A–248.

Name ______________________

Practice 13.4

Add 2 to Numbers 6–8

1

____ + ____ = ____

2

____ + ____ = ____

3

____ + ____ = ____

Directions: 1–3 Write the number in each group. Add. Write the sum.

Copyright © Houghton Mifflin Company. All rights reserved.

Name ______________________

Practice 13.5

Add Pennies

1

______ ______ ______

______ ¢ + ______ ¢ = ______ ¢

2

______ ______ ______

______ ¢ + ______ ¢ = ______ ¢

3

______ ______ ______

______ ¢ + ______ ¢ = ______ ¢

Directions: 1–3 Write the number in each group. Add. Write the sum.

Copyright © Houghton Mifflin Company. All rights reserved.

Name ______________________

Practice 13.6

Practice Addition

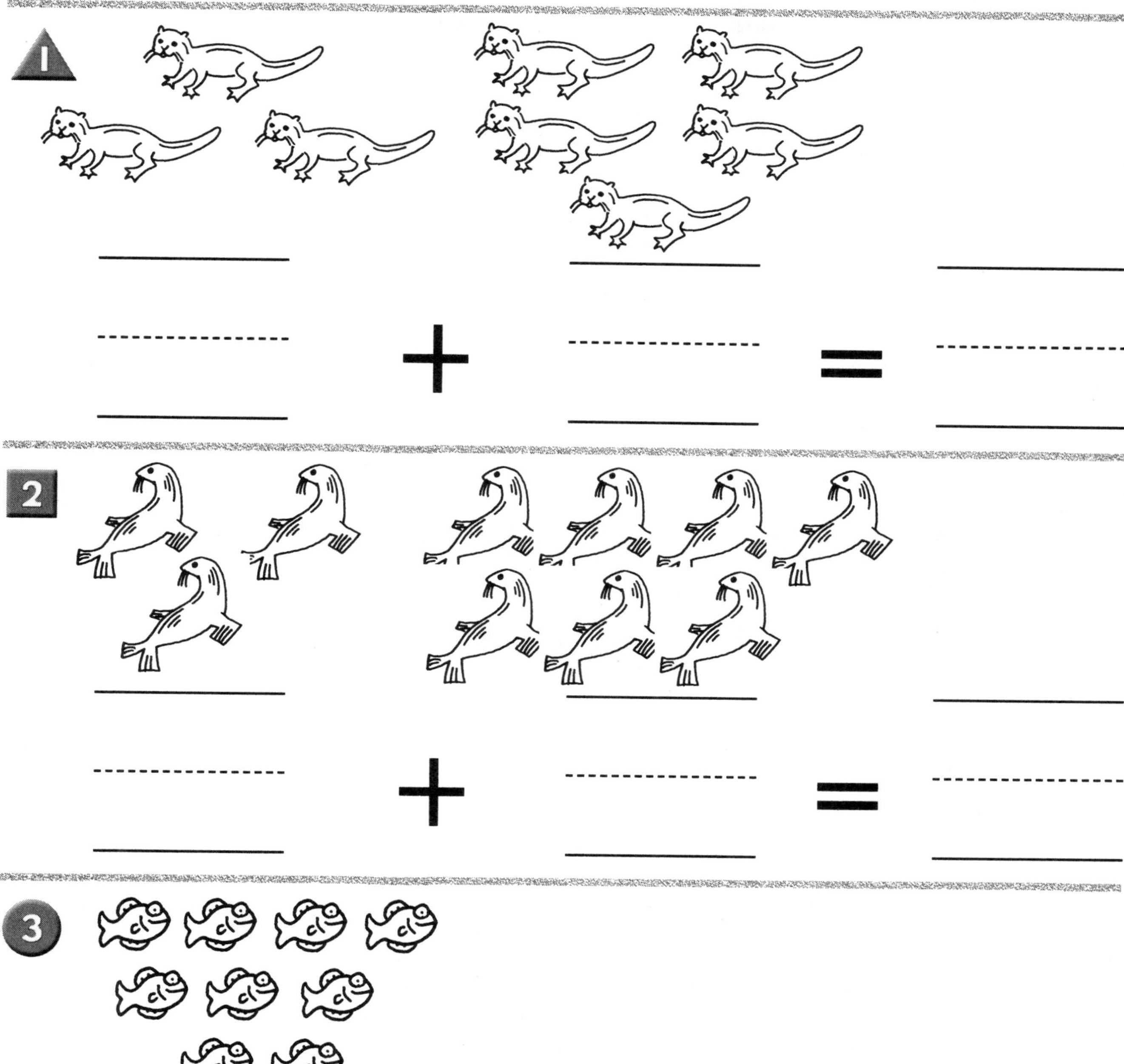

Directions: I–3 Write the number in each group. Add. Write the sum.

Copyright © Houghton Mifflin Company. All rights reserved.

Name ____________________

Practice 13.7

Doubles

1

____ + ____ = ____

2

____ + ____ = ____

3

____ + ____ = ____

Directions: 1–3 Write the number in each group. Add. Write the sum.

Copyright © Houghton Mifflin Company. All rights reserved.

Name ______________________

Practice 13.8

Problem Solving: Draw a Picture

1

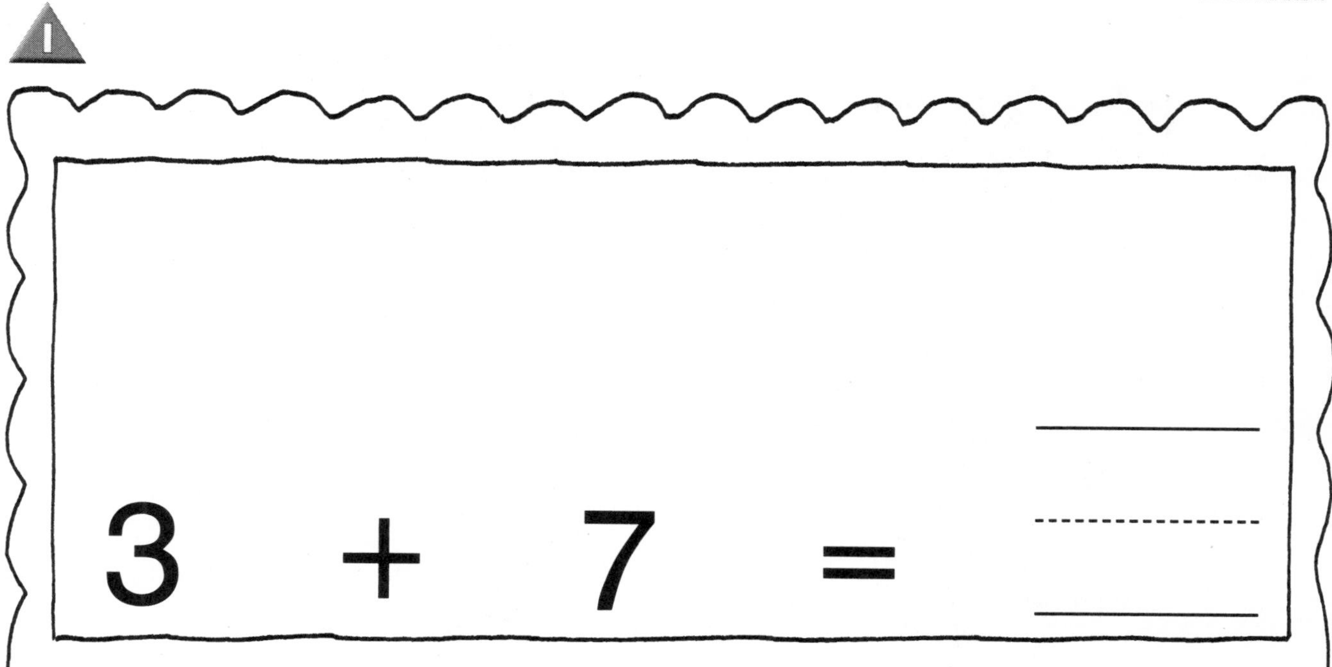

2

3 + 5 = ____

Directions: 1–2 Draw a picture to match the fact. Add. Write the sum.

Copyright © Houghton Mifflin Company. All rights reserved.

Name ___________________________

Practice 14.1

Model Subtraction

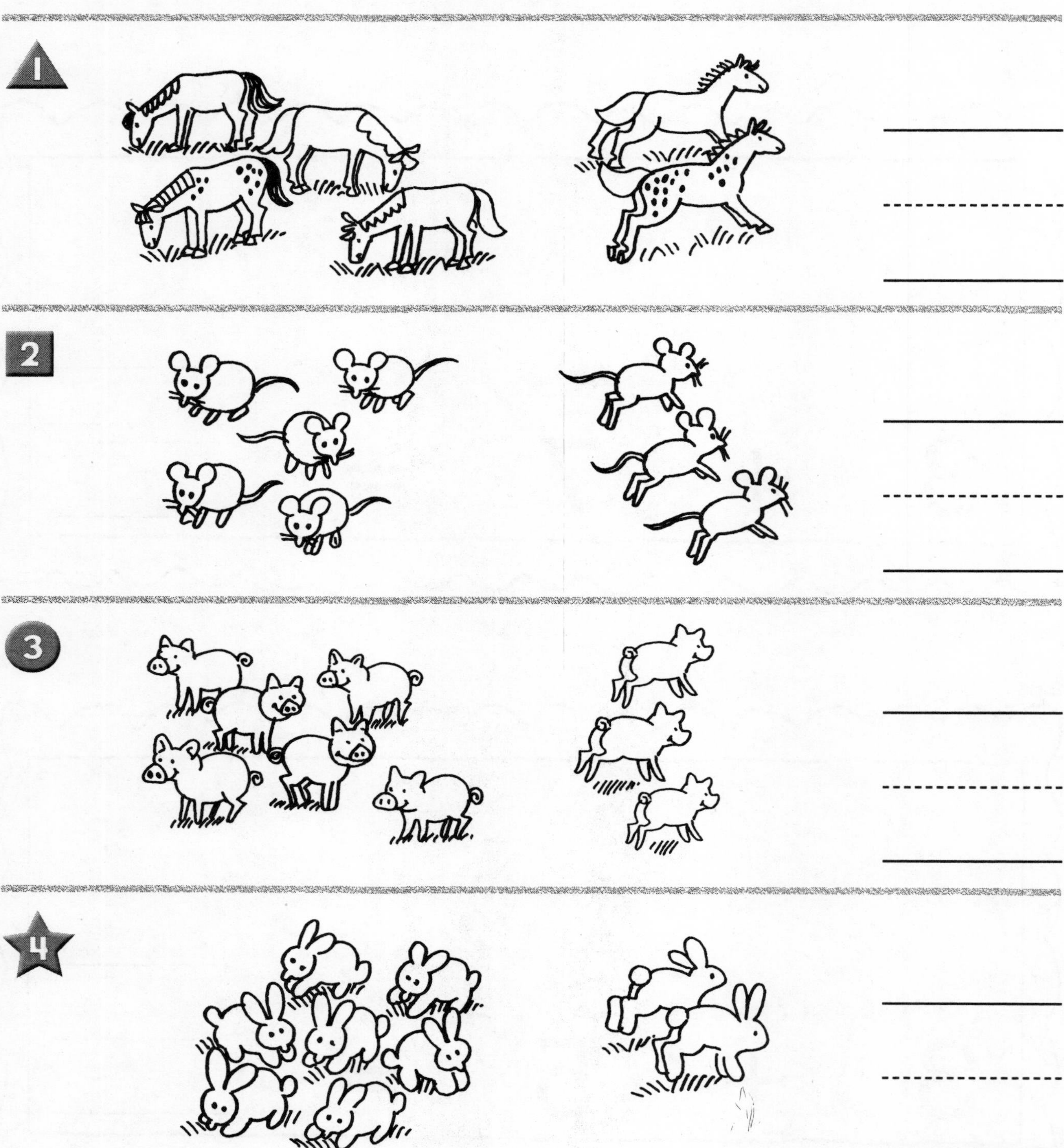

Directions: 1–4 Count how many in all. Circle and cross out the ones that are leaving. Write how many are left.

Copyright © Houghton Mifflin Company. All rights reserved.

Name ______________________

Practice 14.2

Subtract 1 From Numbers 0–9

2

3

Directions: 1–4 Count how many in all. Circle and cross out the one that is leaving. Write how many are left.

Copyright © Houghton Mifflin Company. All rights reserved.

Name ____________________

Practice 14.3

Subtract 2 From Numbers 2–5

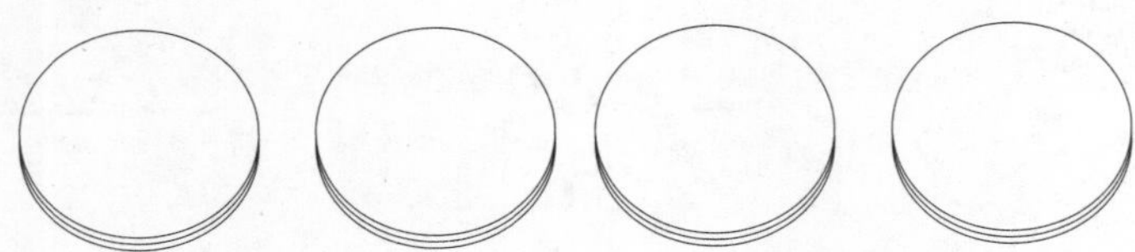

4 − 2 = ____

2

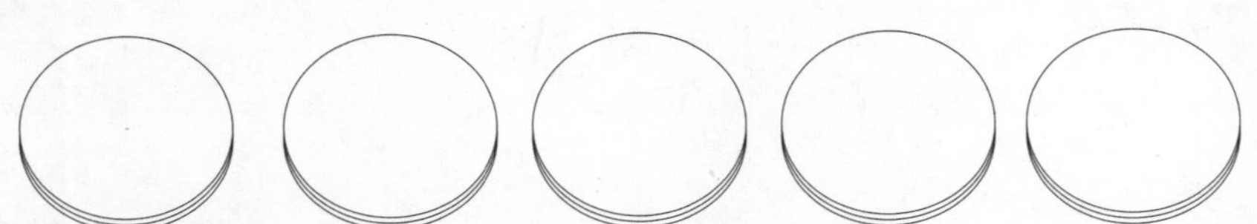

5 − 2 = ____

3

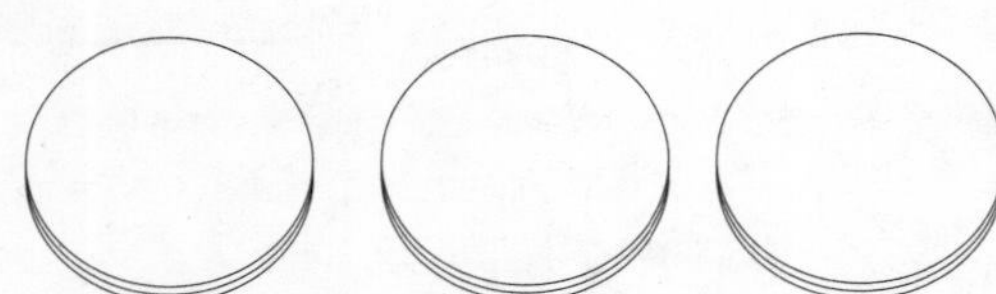

3 − 2 = ____

Directions: 1–3 Show the first number with counters. Take away 2 counters. Circle and cross out the group of 2. Write how many are left.

Copyright © Houghton Mifflin Company. All rights reserved.

Name ______________________

Subtract 2 From Numbers 6–10

1

_____ − _____ = _____

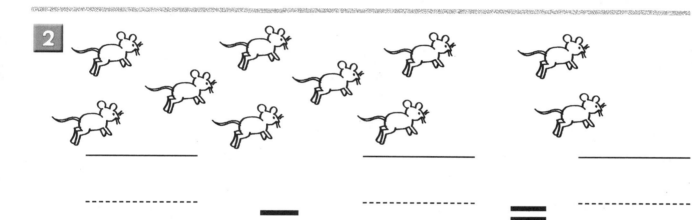

2

_____ − _____ = _____

3

_____ − _____ = _____

Directions: **1–3** Write the number of animals in all. Use counters to model taking away two. Circle and cross out two. Write the number you crossed out. Write the difference.

Copyright © Houghton Mifflin Company. All rights reserved.

Name ______________________

Practice 14.5

Subtract Pennies

1

_____ ¢ − 3¢ = _____ ¢

2

_____ ¢ − 1¢ = _____ ¢

3

_____ ¢ − 2¢ = _____ ¢

4

_____ ¢ − 3¢ = _____ ¢

Directions: **1–4** Count and write the number of pennies in all. Circle and cross out the number shown. Write how many are left.

Copyright © Houghton Mifflin Company. All rights reserved.

Name ______________________

Practice 14.6

Practice Subtraction

______ − ______ = ______

2

______ − ______ = ______

______ − ______ = ______

Directions: 1–3 Write a subtraction sentence to match the picture.

Copyright © Houghton Mifflin Company. All rights reserved.

Name ______________________

Practice 14.7

Relate Addition and Subtraction

1

____ ____ ____

____ − ____ = ____

____ ____ ____

____ + ____ = ____

2

____ ____ ____

____ − ____ = ____

____ ____ ____

____ + ____ = ____

3

____ ____ ____

____ − ____ = ____

____ ____ ____

____ + ____ = ____

Directions: 1–3 Write numbers to complete the number sentence for each picture.

Copyright © Houghton Mifflin Company. All rights reserved.

Name ________________

Practice 14.8

Problem Solving: Choose the Operation

1

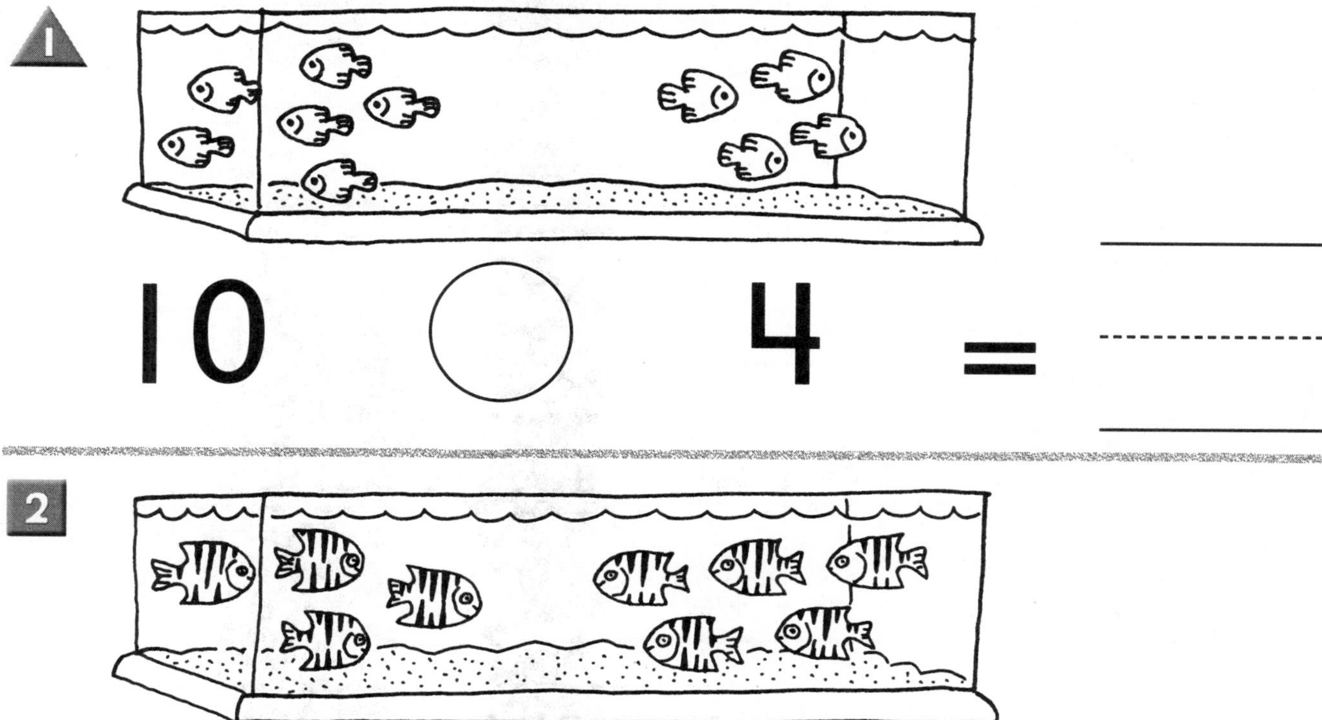

10 ◯ 4 = ____

2

4 ◯ 5 = ____

3

8 ◯ 3 = ____

Directions: **1–3** Tell a story to match the picture. Decide if it shows addition or subtraction. Write a plus or minus sign in the circle. Write the answer.

Copyright © Houghton Mifflin Company. All rights reserved.

Use with Teacher's Edition pages 273A–274.

Name ______________________

Practice 15.1

Numbers 10–12

1 ____

2 ____

3 ____

4 ____

Directions: 1–4 Count the filled ten-frame as 10 and count on. Write the number.

Copyright © Houghton Mifflin Company. All rights reserved.

Name ____________________

Practice 15.2

Numbers 13–14

1

2

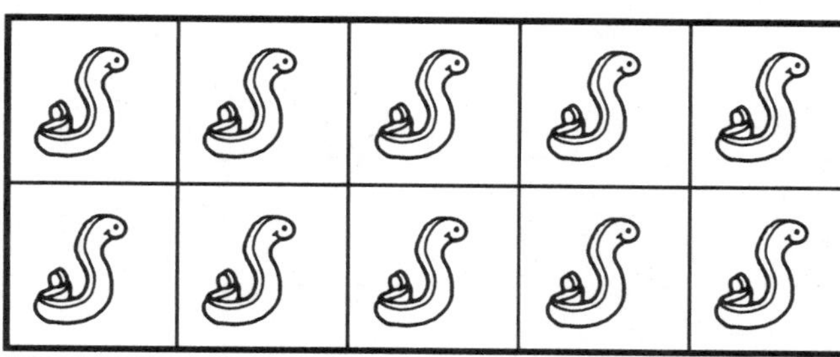

3

4

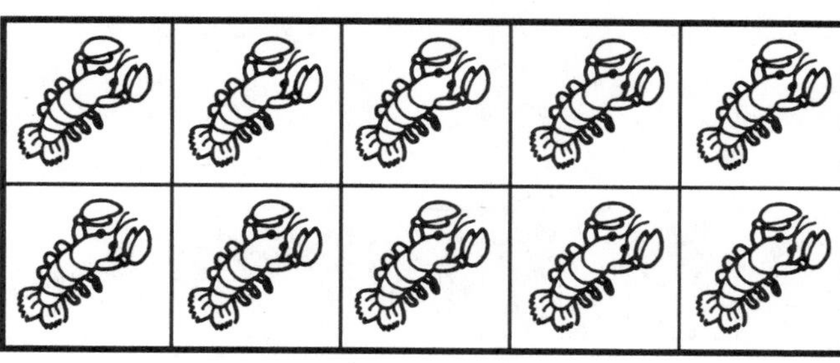

Directions: 1–4 Count the filled ten-frame as 10 and count on. Write the number.

Copyright © Houghton Mifflin Company. All rights reserved.

Name ______________________________

Practice 15.3

Numbers 15–16

14
15
16

2

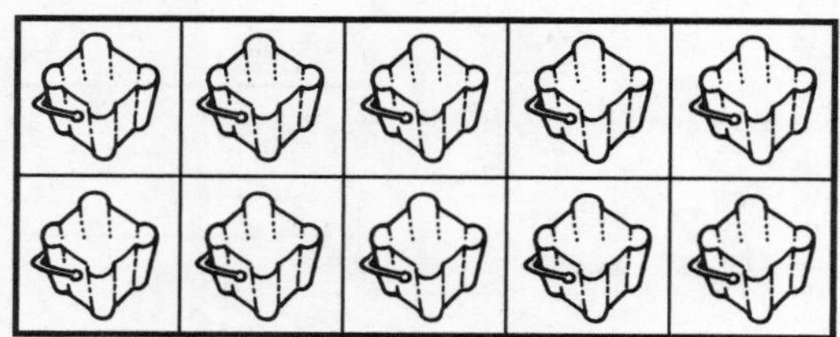

14
15
16

3

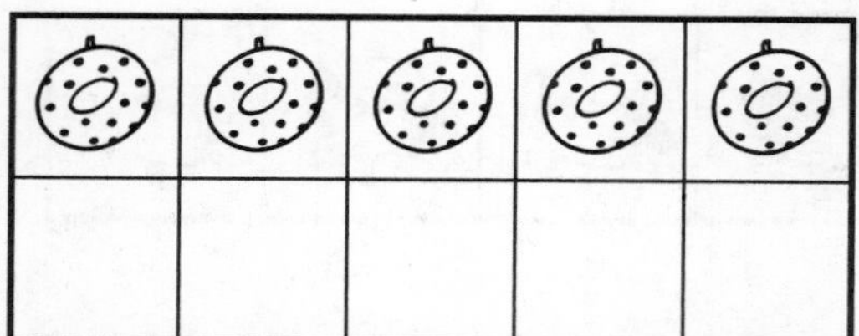

14
15
16

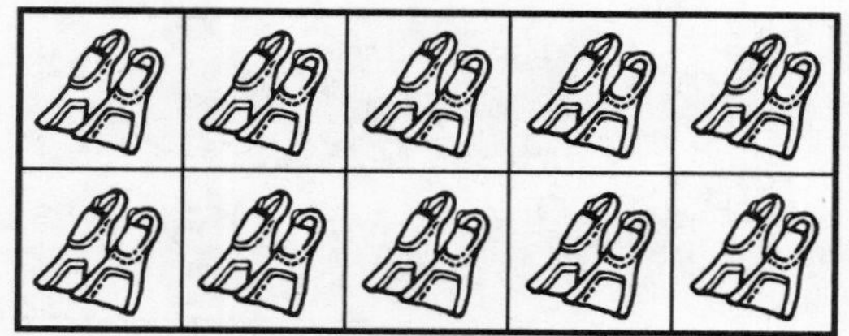

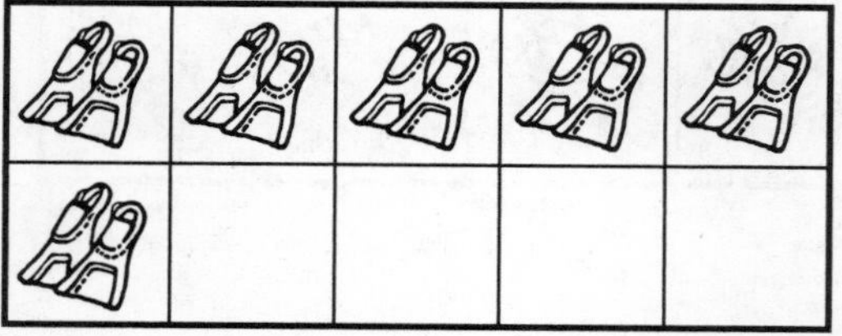

14
15
16

Directions: 1–4 Count the items. Circle the number.

Copyright © Houghton Mifflin Company. All rights reserved.

Use with Teacher's Edition pages 289A–290.

Name ______________________

Practice 15.4

Numbers 17–18

1

17 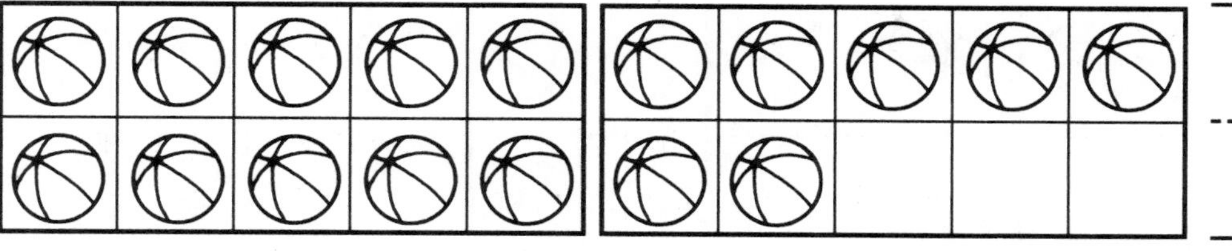

2

18 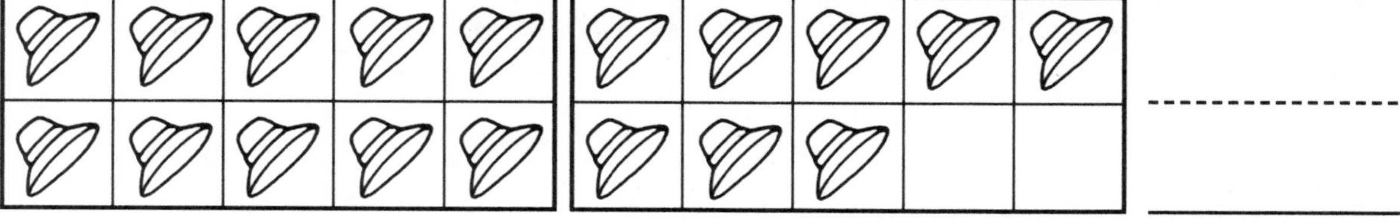

3

18 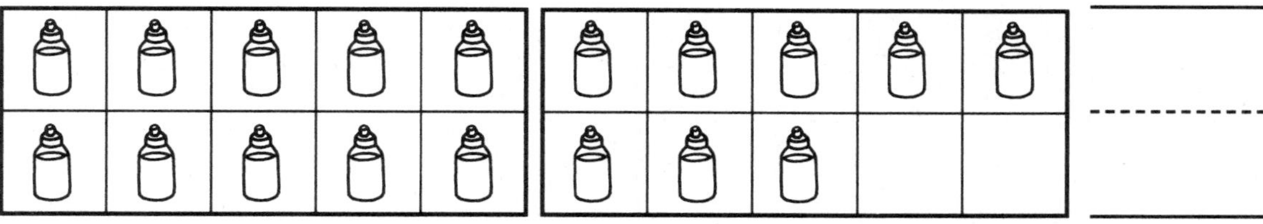

17 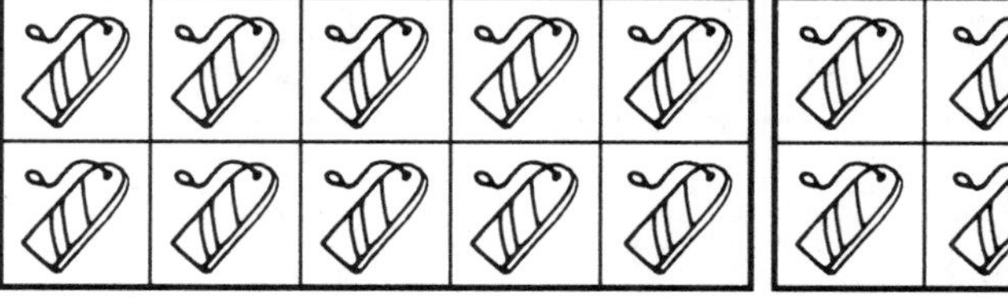

Directions: 1–4 Count the filled ten-frame as ten and count on. Write the number.

Copyright © Houghton Mifflin Company. All rights reserved.

Name ____________________

Practice 15.5

Numbers 19–20

1

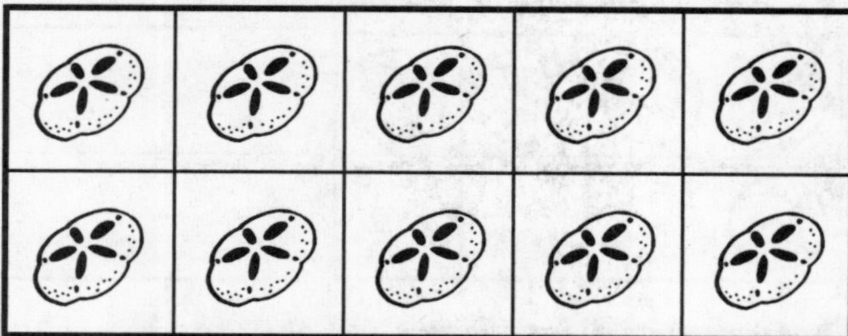

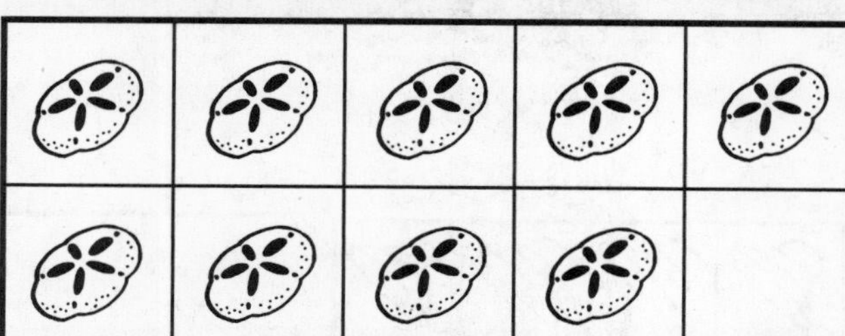

18 19 20

2

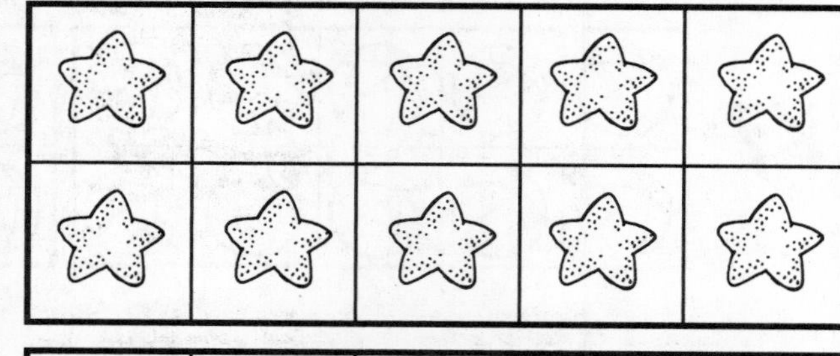

18 19 20

3

18 19 20

4

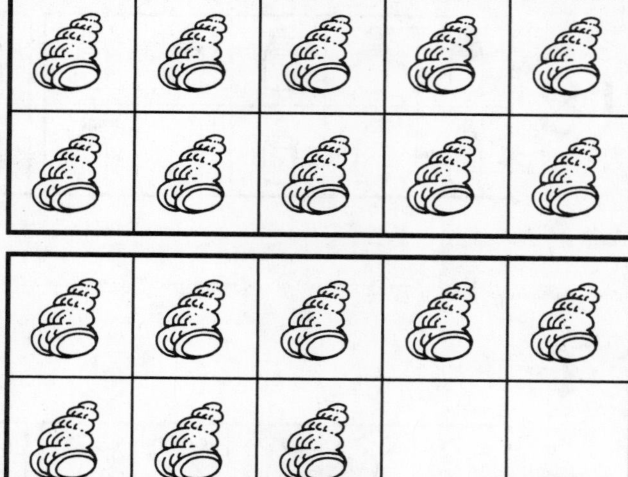

18 19 20

Directions: 1–4 Count the items. Circle the number.

Copyright © Houghton Mifflin Company. All rights reserved.

Name ______________________

Practice 15.6

Order Numbers 10–20

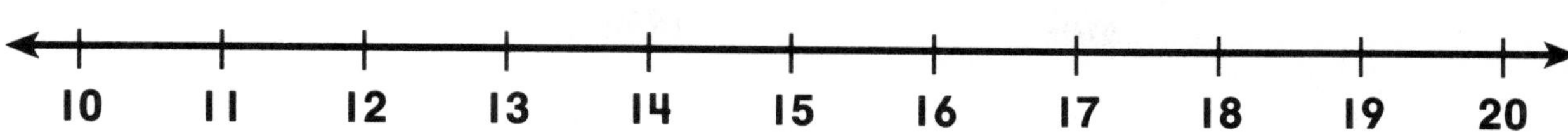

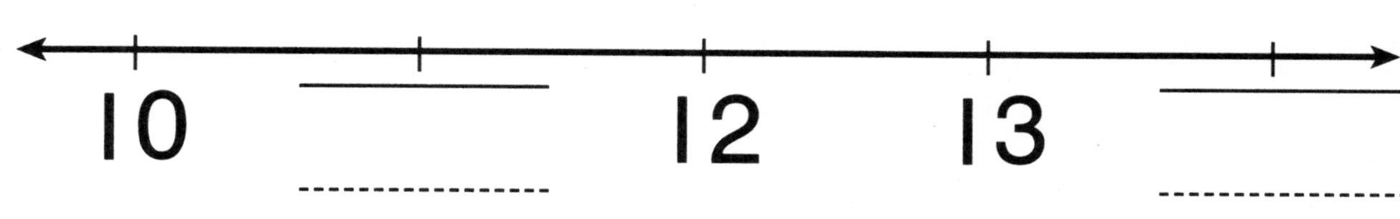

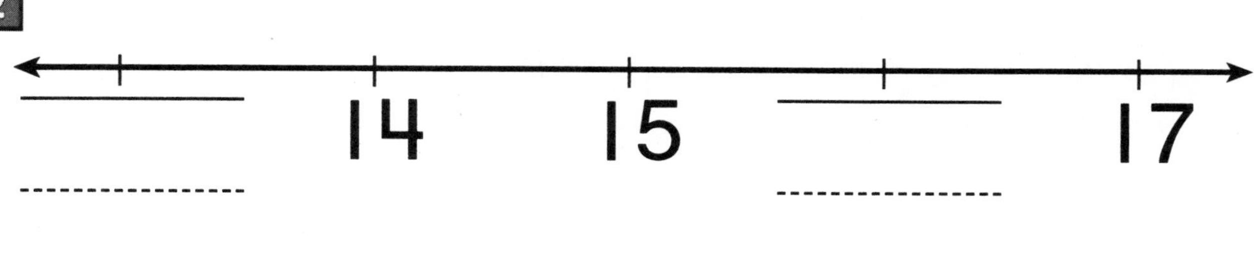

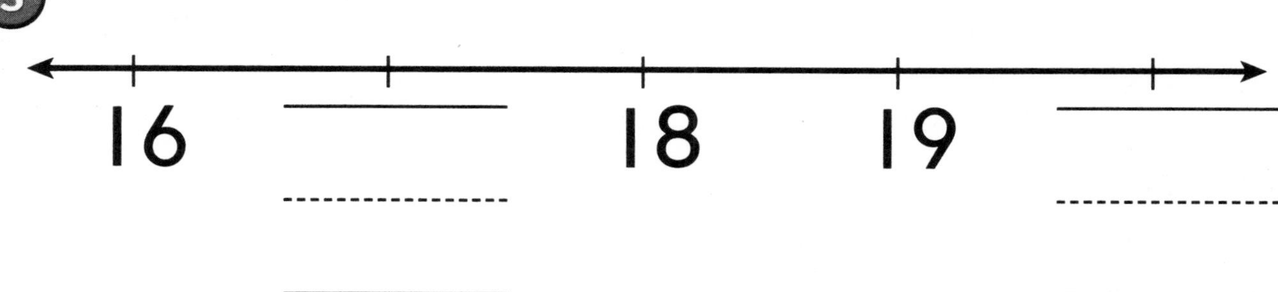

Directions: 1–3 Write the missing numbers.

Copyright © Houghton Mifflin Company. All rights reserved.

Use with Teacher's Edition pages 295A–296.

Name ___________________________

Practice 15.7

Dimes and Pennies

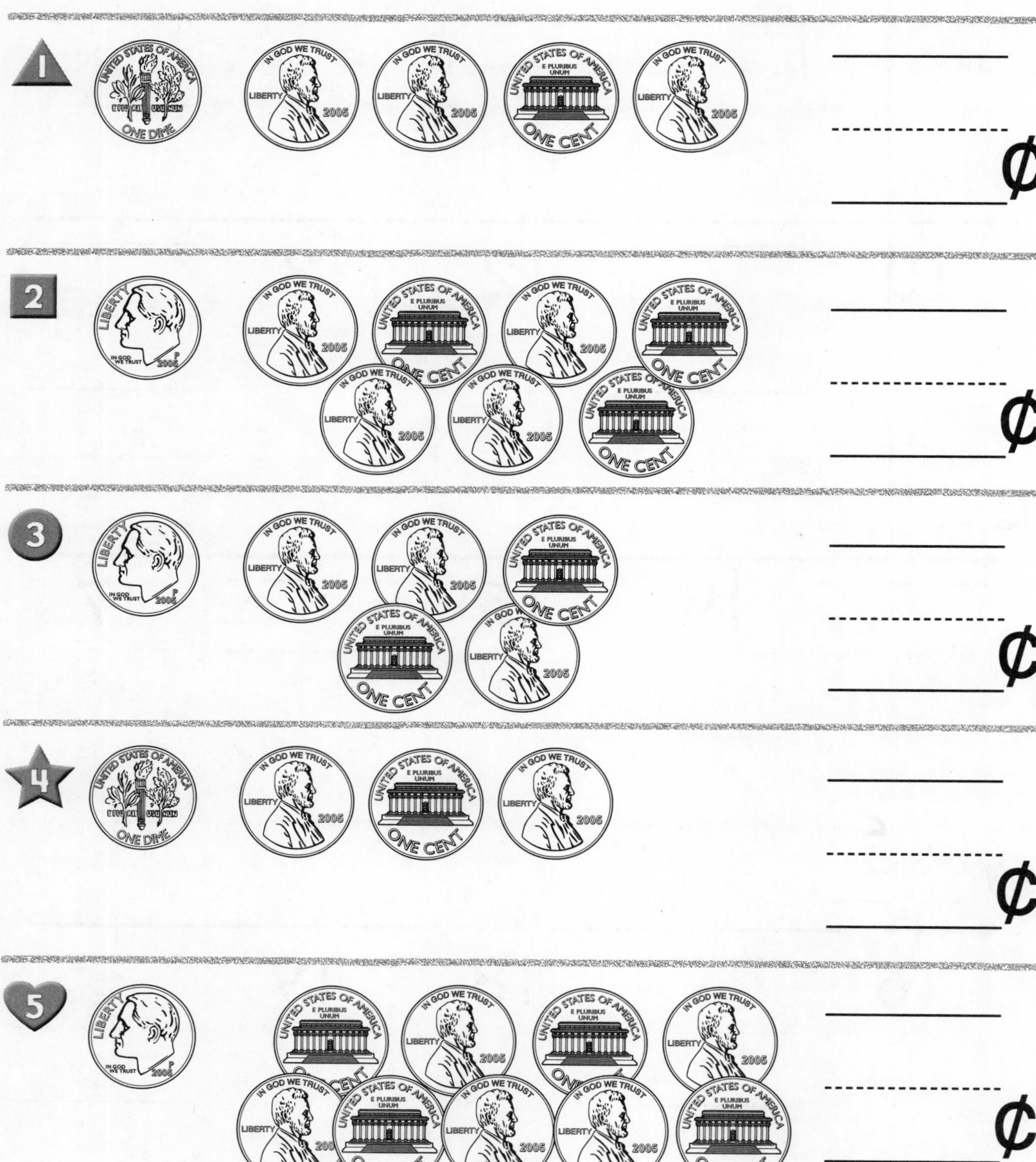

1 ______ ¢

2 ______ ¢

3 ______ ¢

4 ______ ¢

5 ______ ¢

Directions: 1–5 Point to the dime and say "ten cents." Point to each penny as you count on the cents in all. Write the number of cents.

Copyright © Houghton Mifflin Company. All rights reserved.

Name ____________________

Practice 15.8

Estimating

1

10

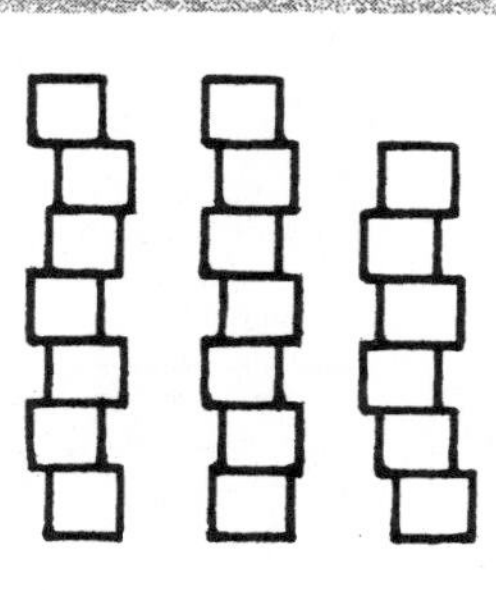

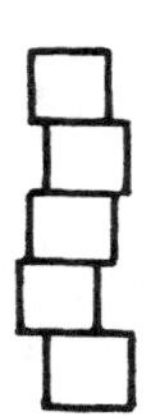

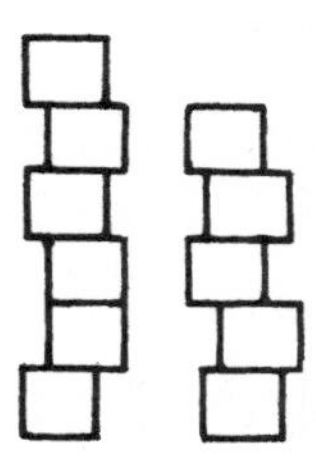

2

15

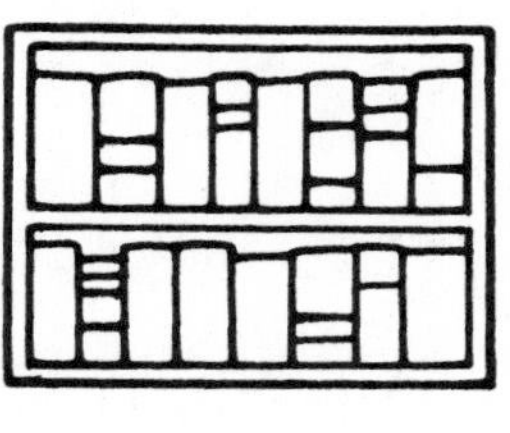

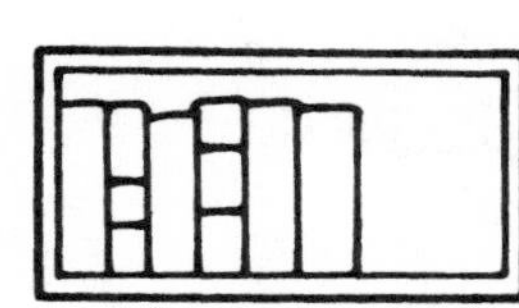

3

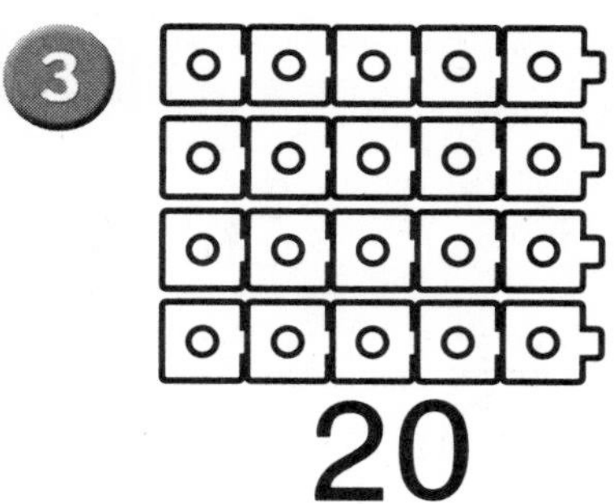

20

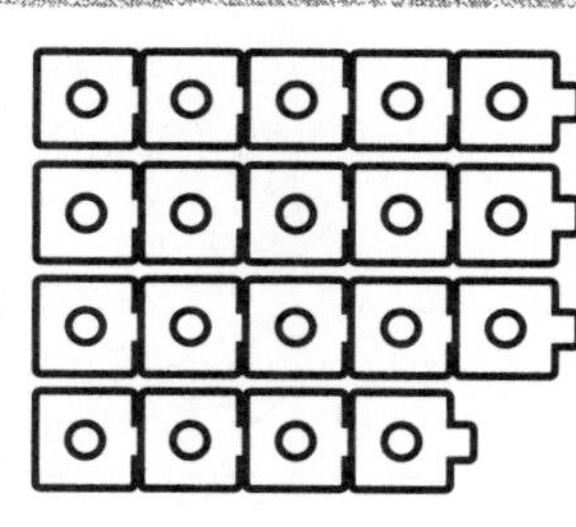

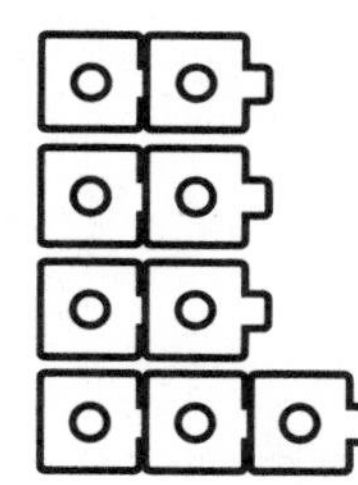

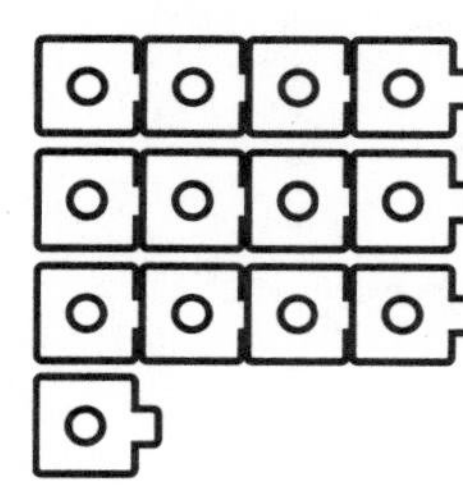

4

15

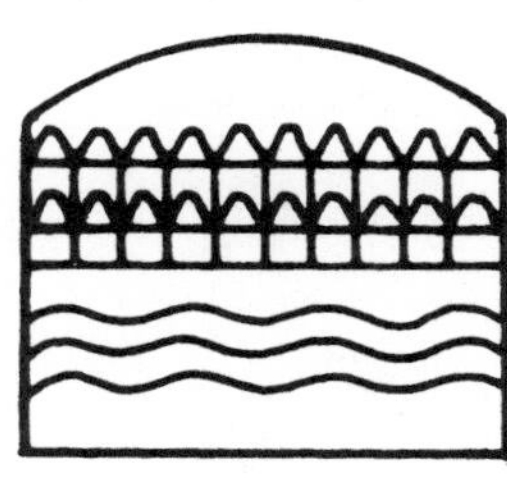

Directions: 1–4 Circle the set that has about the same number as the first set.

Copyright © Houghton Mifflin Company. All rights reserved.

Name ____________________

Practice 15.9

Problem Solving: Guess and Check

1

Guess | Check

more than 15
less than 15

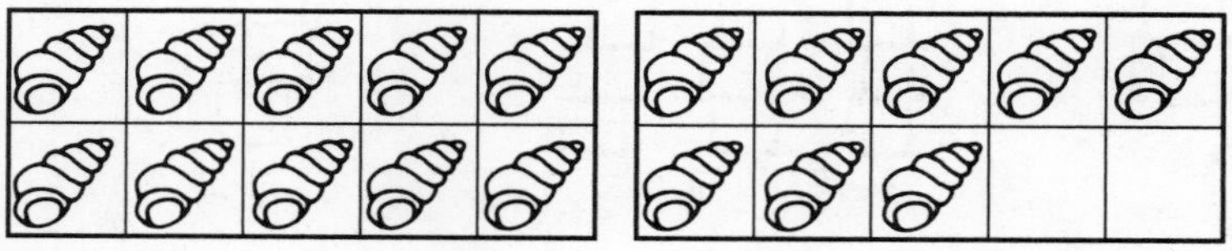

2

Guess | Check

more than 15
less than 15

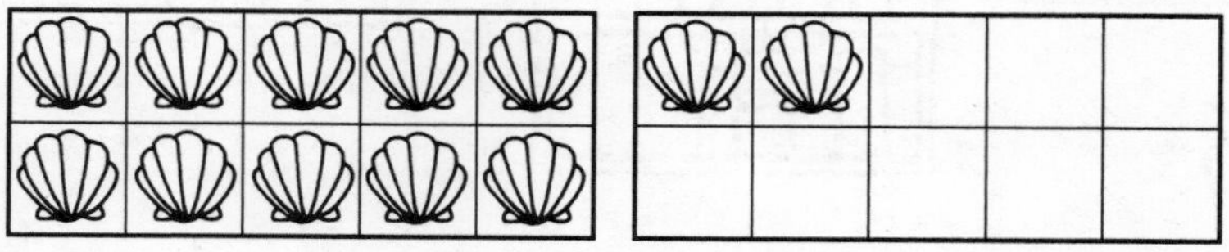

3

Guess | Check

more than 15
less than 15

4

Guess | Check

more than 15
less than 15

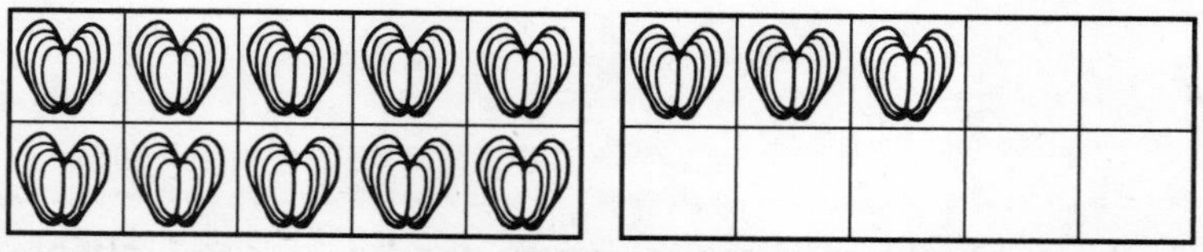

Directions: 1–4 Guess whether the picture shows more than 15 or less than 15. Circle your guess. Count to check your answer. Write the number.

Copyright © Houghton Mifflin Company. All rights reserved.

Name ______________________

Practice 16.1

Numbers 21–25

1

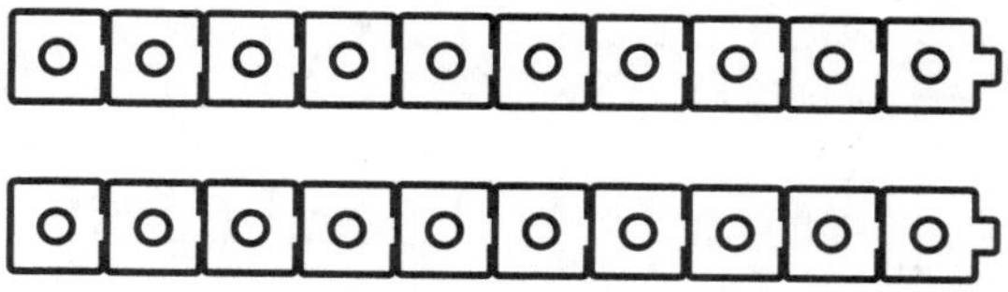

2

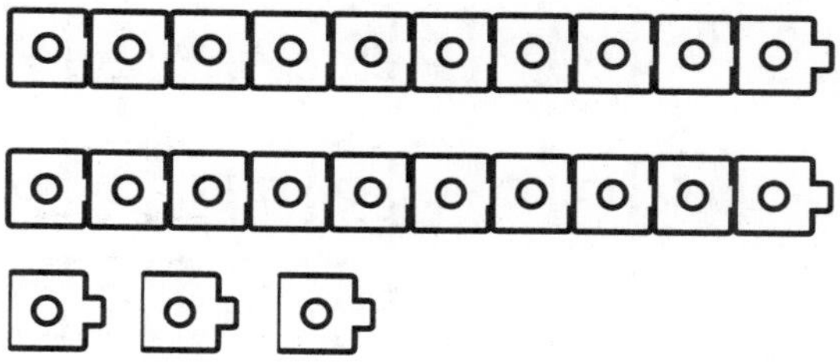

3

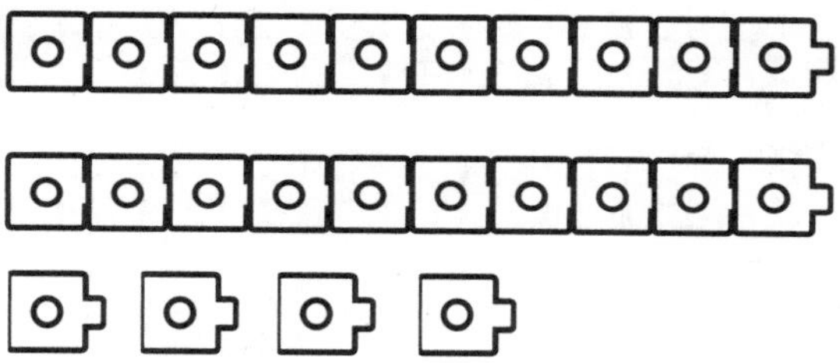

4

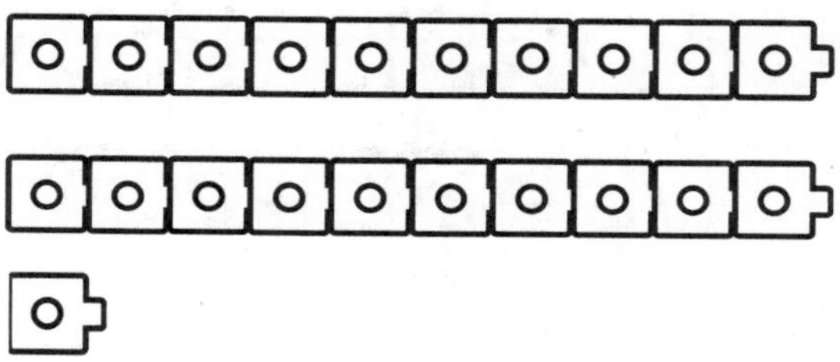

5

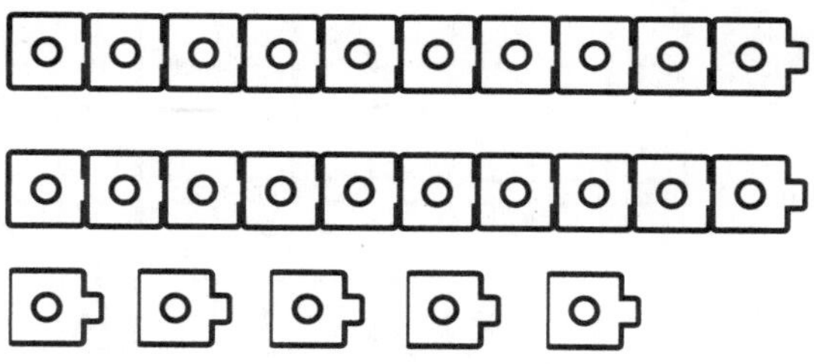

6

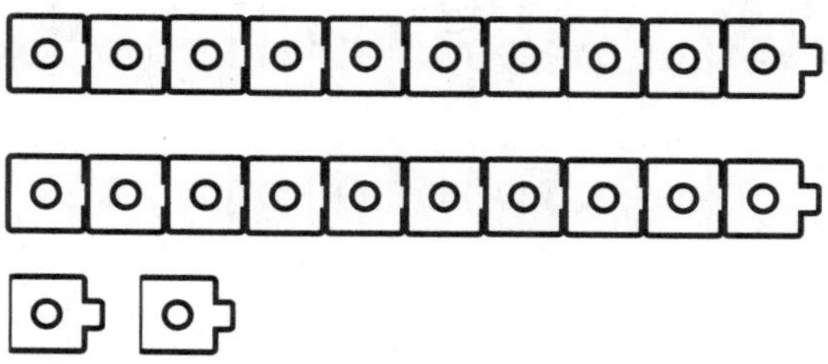

Directions: **1–6** Count the cube trains by tens and then count on. Write the number.

Copyright © Houghton Mifflin Company. All rights reserved.

Use with Teacher's Edition pages 305A–306.

Name ____________________

Practice 16.2

Numbers 26–30

1

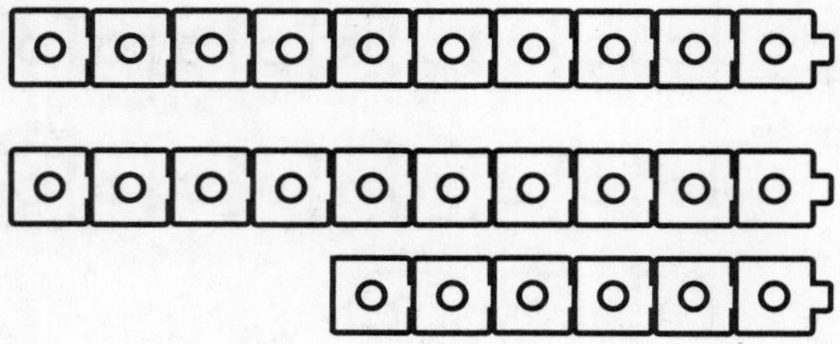

25 26 27

2

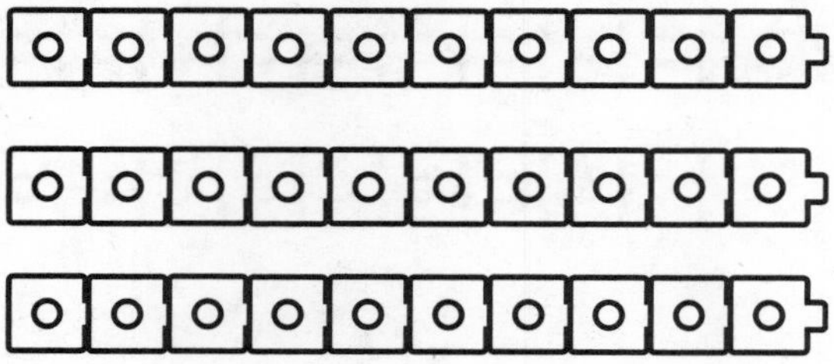

28 29 30

3

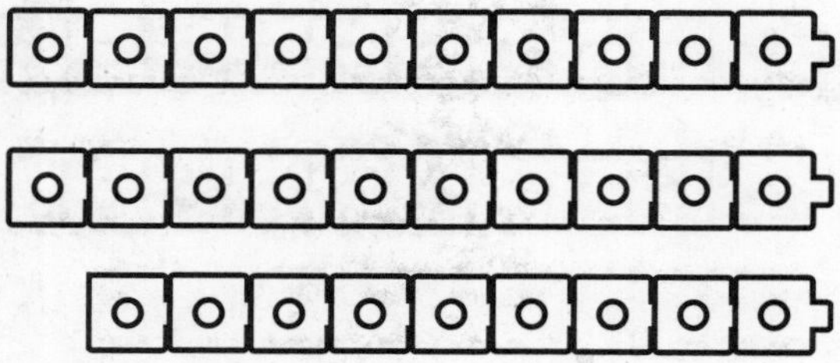

27 28 29

4

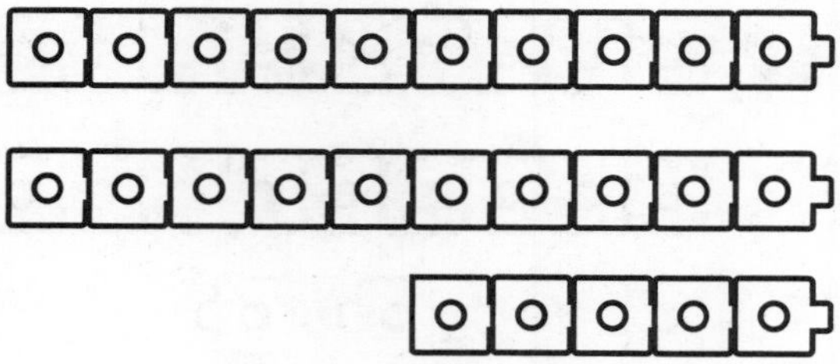

25 26 27

5

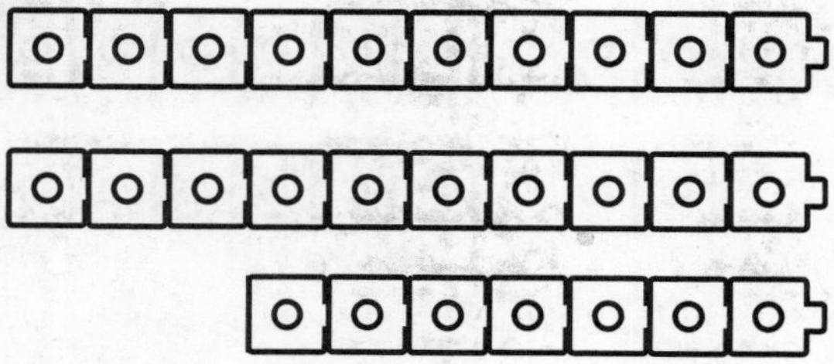

27 28 29

6

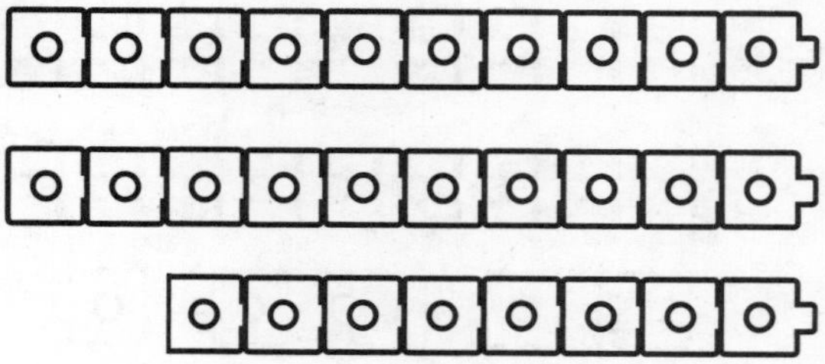

27 28 29

Directions: 1–6 Count the cube trains by tens and then count on. Circle the number.

Copyright © Houghton Mifflin Company. All rights reserved.

Name ____________________

Practice 16.3

Order Numbers 0–31

16 17 18 19 20 21 22 23 24 25 26 27 28 29 30 31

1. ____ 17 ____ 19

2. 20 ____ 22 ____

3. ____ 25 ____ 27

4. 28 ____ 30 ____

Directions: **1–5** Write the missing numbers.

Copyright © Houghton Mifflin Company. All rights reserved.

Use with Teacher's Edition pages 308A–308D.

Name ______________________________

Practice 16.4

Calendar: Using Numbers 1–31

March						
Sunday	Monday	Tuesday	Wednesday	Thursday	Friday	Saturday
	1	2		4	5	
7	8		10	11		13
14		16	17		19	20
	22		24	25		27
28		30				

Directions: Write the missing dates. Then circle each Tuesday. Put an X on the tenth, twentieth, and thirtieth days. Underline the day between the twenty first and the twenty third.

Copyright © Houghton Mifflin Company. All rights reserved.

Name ______________________________

Practice 16.5

Count by Twos, Fives, Tens

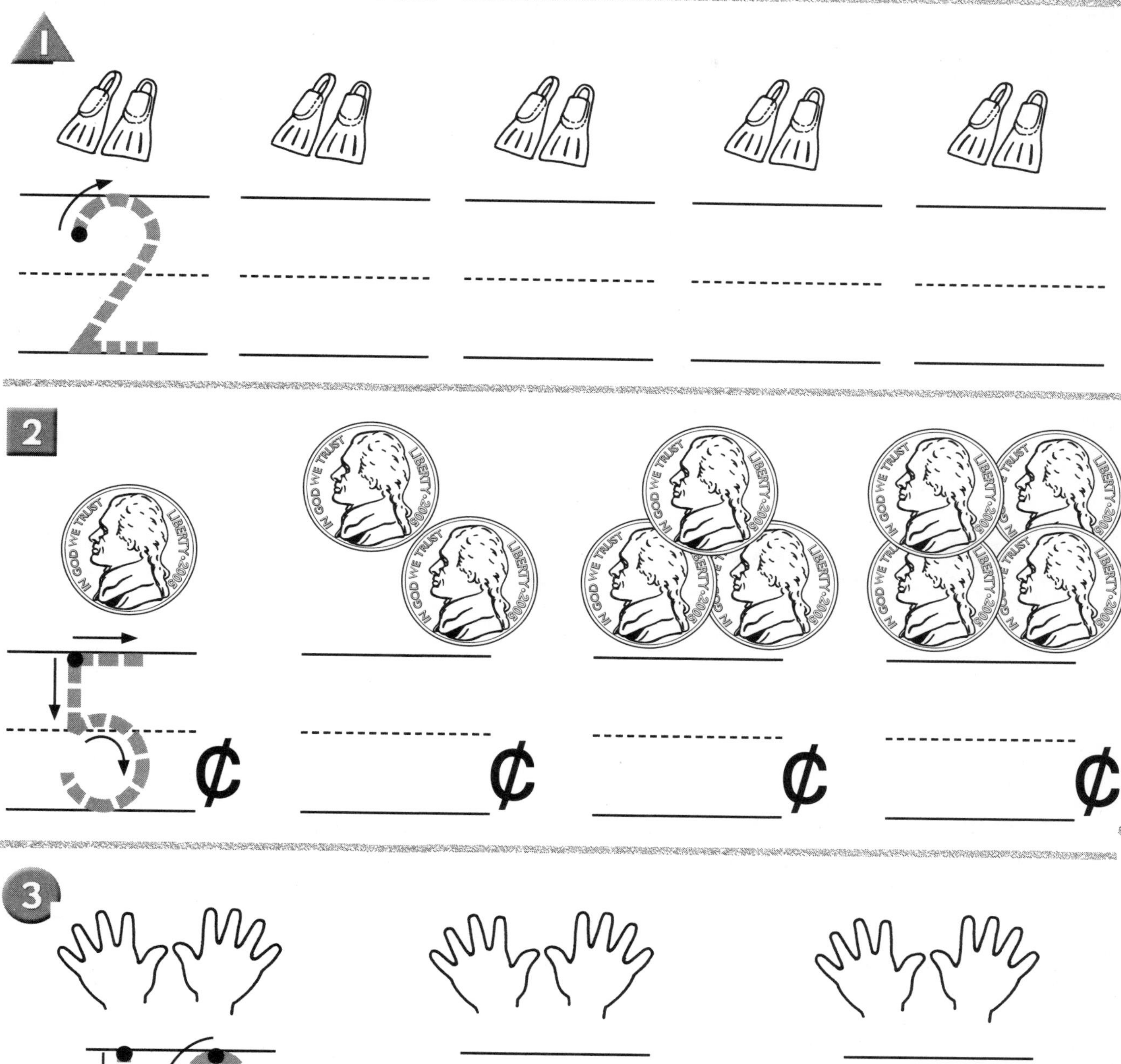

Directions: **1** Count by twos. Write the numbers. **2** Count by fives. Write the numbers. **3** Count by tens. Write the numbers. **4** Count by fives. Write the number of cents.

Copyright © Houghton Mifflin Company. All rights reserved.

Name ______________________

Practice 16.6

Problem Solving: Use a Pattern

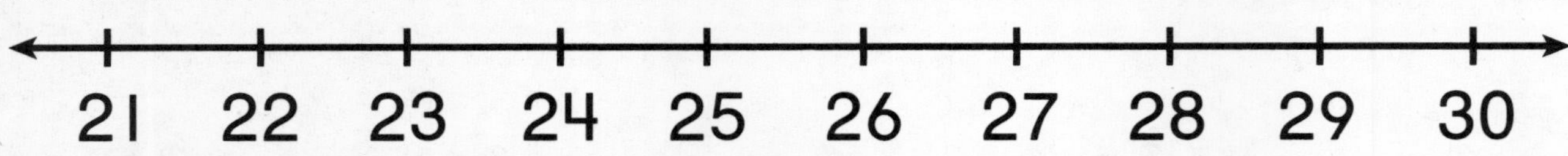

22 ____ 24 ____ 26

2

30 29 ____ ____ 26

3

22 24 ____ 28 ____

4

30 28 26 ____ ____

Directions: 1–4 Look for a pattern. Write the missing numbers. Use the number line to help.

Copyright © Houghton Mifflin Company. All rights reserved.